The

Joyful

Home Schooler

The
Joyful
Home Schooler

Mary Hood, Ph.D.

Cover Designed and Illustrated by

Gaylen Brainard

Ambleside Educational Press

The Joyful Home Schooler

Published by Ambleside Educational Press
P. O. Box 2524, Cartersville, GA 30120

Cover art & additional illustrations by Gaylen Brainard

Printed in the USA

First printing

Printed on acid-free paper

ISBN   0-9639740-6-8

This book is dedicated to all my homeschooling friends. Without your constant support and encouragement, I would not be able to keep on with my work.

Special thanks to my husband and children, who continue to look the other way when I write about things that could prove embarrassing to them. Also, special thanks to Roy Hood and Roxane Olmen for their assistance in editing; to Roxane for her contribution to the chapter on dealing with adversity, and to Gaylen Brainard for her wonderful artwork.

Table of Contents

(Continued on next page)

Table of Contents (continued)

A Personal Note

I receive phone calls every day from mothers who are experiencing either stress or depression. Most of these mothers are homeschooling because they truly believe that the Lord has led them in this direction. All of them genuinely love their children and want to be with them. Yet many are frustrated and have a hard time getting motivated or remaining excited about learning themselves. I found myself wondering why it was that so many women seemed to be having so little fun living a lifestyle that was supposed to be joyful.

As I considered the problem, I remembered a time when I was feeling stressed out and depressed myself. Our family had gone through a series of minor crises that had temporarily thrown me for a loop. I had become irritable, bored, and weary. The daily stresses inherent in balancing household chores and family responsibilities were getting me down. I was having more and more trouble living up to my image as a successful homeschooling mother. For a while, it seemed that all I was doing was getting up in the morning and blundering through the day. A few times, when I was alone in my van, I actually wound up crying. Sometimes I wondered if I was going to have to put the children back in school and forget the whole thing.

At the time, I really didn't know what was wrong, but I did know one thing. The problem was definitely with me. Nobody else was at fault. My husband wasn't doing anything wrong; my children were all fine; and God hadn't changed. He had promised to take the barren women and make them joyful mothers of children, and boy, did I feel barren!

I knew the problem wasn't a lack of salvation. That had been taken care of on the cross, and I had accepted it years ago. My problem was a lack of the "joy of my salvation." That void could only be filled by turning to the Lord and asking Him to help me find my joy and contentment again. I realized that I had let the demands of daily life crowd out my quiet time, and I had been neglecting prayer and Bible study. I had to force myself to make it my number one priority again. Getting up an hour earlier every day, I began to read the Book of Psalms, because I remembered that there were numerous references to joy scattered throughout its pages.

As I studied, I gradually became aware of a pattern that runs all through the Psalms. Do you remember the old hymn that says, "Trust and obey, there's no other way?" That hymn writer must have been studying this book of lyrics. Over and over, the psalmist writes about the need for trust and obedience, coupled with God's promise to bestow joy and blessings on his servants.

When the Psalms were written, God's people were still operating under the "Old Covenant." At that time, obedience meant adherence to a set of specific rules that had been written down in the first five books of the Old Testament. With the coming of the New Testament, this law was fulfilled. It had accomplished its purpose, clearly demonstrating that no man was capable of perfect obedience to a long list of commands. The only way to be "washed as white as snow" is to come to Jesus and believe in the work He did for us on the cross.

We don't have to earn our joy and blessings. They are gifts from God, which are freely given to us when we first come to Jesus and are saved. However, when we don't trust God or fail to obey the personal guidance and correction we receive from the Holy Spirit, we sometimes build barriers that dam up the flow of power and prevent us from enjoying those things that are rightfully ours. God is not the one withholding these things. We are simply failing to appropriate them for ourselves.

I began to realize that the barriers I had constructed through insufficient obedience and trust were preventing me from tapping into His power source. Through recognizing these barriers and tearing them down, one by one, I gradually regained my joy. I hope that this book will help you to find yours, too, if you have temporarily misplaced it.

Psalm 113 promises, "He maketh the barren woman to keep house and to be a joyful mother of children." Barren means "unable to bear children." However, the Bible also uses the word barren to mean "unable to bear fruit." The fruit of the spirit includes "Love, joy, peace, longsuffering, gentleness, goodness, faith, meekness and temperance..." (Gal. 5:22-23). This Psalm was not just directed at the Hannahs of the world, who are physically incapable of bearing children. The Lord also takes those women who feel incapable of bearing the fruit of the spirit and does it for them. He is the giver of joy and "longsuffering," or patience. These are not qualities we have to develop all by ourselves.

When I felt completely empty and incapable of bearing the weight of my responsibilities, all I had to do was to turn everything over to God and let Him handle it for me. As soon as the barriers were removed and I allowed God to take charge of my life, I was able to stop relying on my own puny efforts to control everything and everybody around me. That's when the power and the joy began to flow again for me.

In the first section of this book, we are going to examine some of the most typical causes of stress and depression, and try to find ways to eliminate them from our lives, so we can reclaim the joy we are supposed to have inherited as children of God. In later sections, we will examine the homeschooling situation in detail, and try to find more practical ways to turn our homes into joyful places to live and learn together. However, you don't have to wait until you read the whole book to start feeling joyful! You don't have to wait until you are patient enough to teach your children at home. You don't have to wait until you become more competent. You don't have to wait for your inner contentment to develop. Everything you need to become a joyful home-schooling mother is inside you right now. All you have to do is to peel off any layers you may have placed between yourself and God. If you have any areas of secret disobedience in your life, stop focusing on your own inadequate efforts to be good and ask God to take them away for you. If you stumble again tomorrow, don't feel like there's no hope, but don't plan to stumble. Just pick yourself up, ask for forgiveness, and try again the next day. Stop trying to control everything and everybody around you. Give God control of your life. Learn to let go and trust Him. Trust the Holy Spirit to guide and direct the people in your life, including yourself. The joy and the blessings will return!

Part One:

Reclaiming Our Joy

"He maketh the barren woman to keep house, and to be a joyful mother of children." Psalm 113:9

"Children, obey your parents in the Lord, for this is right. Honour thy father and mother: which is the first commandment with promise; That it may be well with thee and thou mayest live long on the earth. And, ye fathers, provoke not your children to wrath, but bring them up in the nurture and admonition of the Lord." (Eph. 6:1-4)

Chapter One

Learning to Obey

One reason God placed us in families was to help us to understand our relationship with Him. In many ways, we learn about God through our relationship with our earthly father and mother. Without first learning how to obey our parents here on earth, it is much harder to learn the proper way to obey God.

Why do we expect our children to obey us? Other than the clear direction from the Bible, why do we even care whether or not they obey us? The answer, of course, lies in our love relationship with them. We love our children, and therefore want only the best for them. We want them to grow up safely and enjoy good health. We want them to learn how to get along with others and to love and respect their brothers and sisters. We dream of a wonderful future for our children, and set worthwhile goals for them.

In order to help our children stay safe, healthy, and moving forward towards these goals, we set broad guidelines concerning the behavior we expect them to exhibit. In order for them to stay safe, they must learn to follow our commands quickly, without procrastinating. If a young child is about to get hit by a car, and we yell, "Stop!," we don't want that child to take three more minutes to consider whether or not to obey us. In order for our children to remain healthy, we want them to learn to eat proper foods, get sufficient rest and exercise, and dress warmly during the winter.

Most of these rules are laid down in a general manner when the children are very young. From that point on, our role is to train them to follow the rules in a consistent manner. At times this calls for discussions or gentle reminders. At other times, it may require harsher forms of discipline, but such punishments are always motivated by our love for them. Occasionally, new situations may arise that we never thought about before. New rules must be formulated. If the children are a little older, we may sit down and discuss the reasons for the new rules with them, but we certainly don't feel bound by the need to act in a completely democratic manner. After all, we are the ones in charge, and we expect them to obey us.

Now, let's examine what this system of rules must feel like from the standpoint of the child. On the surface, the child probably doesn't appreciate the need for all these rules. "Don't touch that. Put on your coat and hat. No candy before supper. Don't run in the house. Stop arguing. Don't hit your little sister"...Nag, nag, nag! Why do most little children obey all these rules, rather than revolting and running away? Deep down, despite their desire to eliminate the rules, they realize that their parents love them. They know that their parents have developed these rules because of that love, and they trust their parents to do what is right for everybody.

Obedience is also necessary in times of change, when the parents must establish a new direction for the family and the children are too immature to understand the need for the change. The parents often have a vision of the future that the children can't see. Suppose the father has a new job in a town far away from the family's current home. One day, he comes in and announces, "Everybody, time to pack up. We're moving to Atlanta." The children have no reason to be happy about this announcement. They have never been to Atlanta. They like their home. Their rooms are set up just the way they want them. They don't want to leave their friends. They are afraid of making changes, because they don't know what the new experience will be like. However, once again, they believe that their father knows what he is doing. Despite their own misgivings, they trust their parents and have good reason to hope that the future will turn out okay.

For a moment, however, let's take a peek in another home. In this household, the father and mother really don't love their children. They don't particularly want the best for them. They have never sat down and thought out a clear set of guidelines for the family, but simply react when the children make them mad. "Don't do that. Don't touch that. Get out of the room. Go away." These children don't feel loved. They may obey on the surface, but underneath they are rebellious. As soon as they can get away from the criticisms and the yelling, they will do whatever they please. When their father comes in and announces an upcoming move to Atlanta, these children cringe in fear. What new problems will they have to face? Will their father use this opportunity to take them away from their safe existence, where they have learned how to cope with their problems, and drop them off somewhere, leaving them defenseless? These children may go where they are told, but they will go kicking and screaming. They will be worried and fearful, because they do not trust their father, and have no assurance of his love.

Which scenario describes the way you feel about your Heavenly Father? Do you understand how much He loves you? Do you know that His guidance and correction is done for your benefit? Do you believe that He has a plan for your future and has set goals for you to accomplish here on earth? Do you understand that He is leading you through your experiences, even when they seem to be hurtful or pointless? Do you believe that His love will continue to sustain you and lead you to a future that will be bright and shining? Or do you fear the future? Do you worry that He will lead you somewhere and then leave you stranded high and dry? Do you think He is temporarily distracted and doesn't know or care what you are going through?

I remember one time when I was worried that the Lord had temporarily misplaced my family and forgotten where He had left us. My husband had been transferred from Alabama to Maryland. As soon as we arrived, we rented a house with the intention of remaining a few months before buying a new place of our own. Since we didn't plan to stay in the house very long, we overlooked a number of minor items, such as the six-foot ceilings in the upstairs bedrooms, the single dysfunctional bathroom, the mildew that covered the walls, and the stream that flowed right through the basement, complete with crawdads and frogs.

Two years later, after exhausting every real estate firm in a six-county area, we began to realize that we might have made an error in selecting that particular short-term rental. At that point, we began to pray fervently for another transfer, but it seemed long in coming. Finally, I prayed the prayer of relinquishment. "Lord, I'm willing to stay right here in this drafty, damp house, if you can convince me that it's your will, but I need something concrete. When Moses was supposed to stay in one spot, you gave him a pillar of smoke. I want one, too. Show me a pillar of smoke on this property, and I will stay here for as long as you wish."

Later that afternoon, I was vacuuming the downstairs when suddenly the vacuum cleaner blew up. There was a beam of sunshine streaming in the window and it illuminated a very distinct column of smoke and debris standing right in the middle of my living room. The children rushed in to find their mother collapsed on the floor in hysterics. It was a nice reminder that the Lord not only knows exactly where I am at all times and has a plan for my life, but He also possesses a keen sense of humor!

"'For I know the plans I have for you', declares the Lord, 'plans to prosper you and not to harm you, plans to give you a hope and a future' " (Jer. 29:11). Do you believe that your Father has a plan for your life? Do you trust Him to bring it to pass? Do you really understand how much He loves you? Without the belief that your Father loves you, obedience has a hollow ring. Why would you continue to obey a master that you couldn't trust? You would obey when you thought he was looking, but as soon as you thought you could get away with something, you'd be sure to turn away from him.

What do you think your job as a parent would be like if you could get your young children to understand the depth of your love for them? What if you could get them to understand the reason for all the rules? What if somehow they could comprehend your underlying concerns? If you could somehow accomplish that, you wouldn't have to focus on the need for specific rules, because the children would know how to act on their own! If they really understood about safety, they would stop running out in the road and playing with matches. If they really understood the need for good health, they would put aside the candy and eat good food. They would automatically stop and put on their hat and coat before they went outside. If they really loved their brothers and sisters as much as Jesus loved them, the arguing would stop. Of course, they still wouldn't be perfect. None of us are. They would still make mistakes, even if they had the best of intentions. However, your role would certainly be a lot easier if you had their full cooperation. You would simply continue to demonstrate your love for them, remind them of rules occasionally when they forgot, and continue to provide guidance and direction for their lives.

That is precisely the role of the Holy Spirit in the life of the believer! The broad guidelines have already been given to us in the Bible. The reminders, daily guidance, and new teachings come from the Holy Spirit, which is that portion of God that resides inside of us. The occasional punishments and times of testing are rooted in God's love for us, and are meant for our refinement and ultimate benefit, not for our demise. God is always the one in charge, whether we realize it or not. Sometimes, He has to remind us of that. When we disappoint him with our behavior or lack of trust, we are not only thwarting our own joy, but blocking His joy, too. He rejoices greatly when He sees our obedience and trust in Him, because He loves to pour out blessings and joy on His people. He hates it when we erect barriers that prevent us from receiving His gifts.

The true believer, who has a portion of God inside him in the person of the Holy Spirit, doesn't have to question the basic love of God. He doesn't have to worry or fear the future. He doesn't have to try to control everything or everyone around him. He doesn't have to try to meet everybody else's needs on his own strength. He doesn't have to follow a million confining rules and criticize everybody else who fails to obey them, either, because he knows that such rules are no longer necessary.

Just like children who grow up and no longer need a long list of rules to control their behavior, those of us who live under the New Covenant no longer need such a list. Instead, we can rely on the Holy Spirit to guide and direct our actions and our thoughts. (Galatians 2:19-21; 3:24-26; 5:18). We know that, no matter what the future may hold, we have a Heavenly Father who is all-powerful and loves us with a perfect love.

If you have trouble feeling the love of your Heavenly Father surrounding you on a daily basis, get down on your knees right now and ask God for the faith to believe in that love. Give Him your will and ask Him to supply the emotion for you. If you ask for faith and the ability to feel His love, He will supply it.

> *"What man is there of you, whom if his son ask bread, will he give him a stone? Or if he ask a fish, will he give him a serpent? If ye, then, being evil, know how to give good gifts unto your children, how*

much more shall your Father which is in heaven give good things to them that ask him?"
(Matt. 79-11)

The real key to getting back your joy and eliminating worry and fear from your life forever is to learn to bask in God's personal love for you, His child. You know what it feels like to love a child. Your Father loves you even more than you love your own children. If you were given total power to control the lives of your children, you know you would help them in every way that you could. You have a Father Who has that ability! If you can just comprehend the depth of His love for you, and understand the limitless resources and power He has at His disposal, what could you possibly find to worry about anymore? Pray and ask the Lord to show you how much He loves you. Claim that love for yourself. Re-discover the joy of your salvation!

"This one thing I do: forgetting those things which are behind and reaching forth unto those things which are before, I press toward the mark for the prize of the high calling of God in Christ Jesus."
(Philippians 3:13-14)

Chapter Two

Trusting God with the Past

Perfect trust in God cannot coexist with a preoccupation with the past. We live in an age that has become permeated with the ideas of psychiatry. Psychiatrists tell us that our past life has conditioned our present. The past must be dredged up and dissected. It isn't enough to do it once, either. It must be done over and over again, in weekly sessions, lying on the psychiatrist's couch. "Now let's talk about your relationship with your mother." "Okay, what else did your father do to you when you were a child?"

The Bible tells us that the past is over. Period. When you become a Spirit-filled Christian, you become a new person. "Therefore if any man be in Christ, he is a new creature: old things are passed away; behold all things become new." (II Cor. 5:17) When my brother and I were little, we used to play a game of shoot-em-up. As soon as one of us hit the ground, pretending to be dead, we would bounce back up, shouting, "New person!" and go on with the game. That's what Jesus does for us. He makes us each a new person when we come to Him and ask Him into our hearts.

It sounds easy, because it is easy, if you let Jesus do it for you. It's only when you insist on trying to become a new person on your own power that it becomes downright impossible. You can't become a "new person in Christ" if you are hanging on with all your strength to something in the past. What is bogging you down today? Is it an abusive parent? A former love? A period of time when you were single and free? Do you go back in your mind and relive the same old episodes again and again? Let go and let God put your past in the past where it belongs. Only then will you really be free to live your present life in the fullness of His joy.

"Oh, Mary,"... I hear some of you sighing, "I'd love to do that. I've tried and tried, but you just don't understand. If you only knew what my past was like, you'd understand." Maybe I don't understand, but Jesus does. Tell Him about it! Just remember that Jesus is not a psychiatrist. He doesn't want you to lie on His couch and tell Him the same garbage every week. Do it one more time, and let Him heal you forever.

One of the hardest things for any woman to put behind her is a failure in the relationship with her earthly father. Many women tell me that they can't get close to men or feel close to their Heavenly Father because they didn't have an earthly one who loved them. Well, neither did I. Oh, I suppose my dad might have loved me deep down, but he never showed it to me. Among other things he gave me as his legacy were such statements as, "No one will ever want to marry you" ... "You would be pretty good-looking if you were a little thinner" ... "People like us don't go to college..." I remember bouncing downstairs as a small child and being deliriously happy just to see my father standing at the foot of the stairs. "Hi, daddy!", I called out. His reply was, "If you can't think of something intelligent to say, don't say anything at all."

For many years, these statements drove my behavior. Such treatment might have caused some people to shrivel up and become introverts. Instead, I adopted an "I'll show him" philosophy, which persisted long after my father's death. "Can't go to college, huh? Well, watch me get these graduate degrees!" "Nobody will ever love me, huh? Just see how popular I can be!" But I never felt popular or loved and I was never satisfied with my academic or worldly success until I met my true Father and discovered the key to overcoming these negative emotions.

I had to deal with the issue of forgiveness before complete healing could take place. I had to be willing to forgive my earthly father before my Heavenly Father could forgive me and help me to move forward with my own life. The forgiveness itself took place quickly, as soon as I turned to Jesus and let Him know that I meant business. However, the emotions took much longer to pull into line. I had been hurt so badly for so many years that a total emotional healing seemed like an impossible task, but "With God all things are possible" (Matthew 20:26).

In *Tramp for the Lord*, Corrie Ten Boom talked about a similar experience. After witnessing the horrors of a concentration camp, she was able to go on with her life without bitterness because she understood the need for putting the past behind her. Although she thought she had already forgiven her enemies, she found herself face to face one day with one of her former captors, and discovered the hatred that still burned in her heart. On that Sunday morning in post-war Germany, a man came up to her after her talk, beaming, and told of his own conversion to Christianity. "Fraulein," he said, with his arm extended, "Will you forgive me?"

Corrie reported that she stood stock still for what seemed like ages. She had just spoken of forgiveness. She knew that the Bible required forgiveness of others before our own sins can be forgiven. Even knowing that, she couldn't do it! She thought of her own sister's death; the days when they had walked naked past this very guard; the humiliation they had suffered. She just couldn't do it! She couldn't forgive the man!

"Jesus," she prayed, "I can lift my hand. I can do that much. You supply the feeling." In the very next moment, as she lifted her hand, Jesus did supply the emotion. Corrie reported that supernatural warmth flooded her arm, and then her heart, as she was filled with love for this new creation that had once treated her so poorly.

Of course, it may be easier to forgive those who, like this guard, have truly repented of their sins. It was hard for me to forgive my own father, who apparently never did change. Yet I also knew I had to do this in order to escape my own past. I had the desire and determination to forgive him, but my emotions didn't seem to want to cooperate at first. One thing that helped me was a suggestion I read in a magazine article. The author suggested that we re-play hurtful scenes in our minds, while picturing Jesus standing nearby, watching silently. The author told us to imagine ourselves in Jesus' shoes, watching the scene. Realizing that there was Someone present during those difficult times Who loved me and loved my father helped me to see him with a different perspective. Watching my father through Jesus' eyes, I finally learned to love and forgive him, too. It didn't necessarily happen the first time that I did this. The Bible says we are to forgive people "seventy times seven" if necessary. (Matt. 18:22)

Every time a scene from my childhood came to my mind, I had to remind myself of my decision to forgive my father and everyone else involved. Eventually, my emotions began to heal, and the love I felt for my father as a small child was completely restored. Unfortunately, he passed away twenty-five years ago, and will probably never be able to rejoice with me. However, there is no such thing as a one-sided relationship in God's kingdom. Even if my father has lost his chance to enter Heaven and stand at my side someday, my forgiveness must somehow touch him wherever he is.

Maybe you've never had to deal with an abusive parent. Maybe your childhood and youth were happy times. Unfortunately, fond memories can sometimes chain us to the past just as effectively as painful ones. Do the problems of present-day life ever get you down? Do you retreat in your mind to another place and time, one where you were young and free; a time when there were fewer demands and you could actually take a bath without an audience of appreciative toddlers? Well, I've been there, too!

Before I met my husband, I was a carefree, single woman, living a life that many people only dream about. I was a musician in a popular band, had my own apartment and a host of willing suitors, and could come and go as I pleased. During the toddler years, I would often get bogged down with loneliness and diapers. Then, "just for a little while," I'd go into my room, close the door, and relive those happy days. This type of memory is very dangerous. It ranks right up there with a fascination with romance novels or soap operas, or a fixation on a particular movie star. Such fantasies can never compare with your present-day life, which has plenty of blemishes if you look hard enough. The men in your memories do only what you want them to do. They never smell bad or burp. They have long, pleasant conversations with you. They can do everything exactly the way you want them to. Guess who suffers in comparison? Your husband can never compete with these perfect men from your memories! There is no way your present life can seem happy and fulfilled when compared with a dream world that you made up, or that no longer exists.

Good or bad, the past is past. There is no way you can change anything. There is no way to go back. The only place to go is forward. You have to "let go and let God" if you ever want to become a joyful mother of children in your present world. Decide right now to let go of your past forever. Do it today!

"For God hath not given us the spirit of fear; but of power, and of love, and of a sound mind." (2 Tim 1:7)

Chapter Three

Trusting God with the Future

Perfect trust in God cannot coexist with a fearful view of the future, either. The Bible tells us, over and over, that fear is a "spirit," (2 Tim 1:7) which needs to be "cast out" and removed. It reassures us that "perfect love casts out fear" (1 John 4:18).

If we were perfectly confident that our Father loved us and wanted only good things for us; if we knew that we were doing our best to live up to His desires and commands, and if we also understood that He has complete power over all our circumstances, the knowledge of His powerful, all-encompassing love should cast away all fear for all time. The problem is, our knowledge of His love is far from perfect.

Fear of the future is rooted in three things: feelings of unworthiness, a preoccupation with self, and past experiences. As a young bride, I was constantly fearful for my husband's safety. He had to commute thirty miles to work every day, and each day I would wonder if he would make it home in one piece. There were several reasons for this unnatural fear. First, I felt unworthy of my husband's love. My father's words were still ringing in my ears, "No one will ever want to marry you. No one will ever love you." Deep down, I must have thought some mistake had been made, and that the fates were bound to notice soon and make corrections. Second, I was overly concerned with my own needs. I really wasn't worried that my husband was going to die. I was worried that I was going to be left all alone. This worry was undoubtedly enhanced by the fact that most of the women who were close to me had been widowed early in life. Therefore my past experiences were also conditioning my present fear.

If you possess any similar anxieties and fears, you must deal with these three issues to order to eliminate the cause of your insecurity. To begin with, you must try to understand the depth of your Father's love for you, so you can begin to believe that you actually deserve the good things you have been given. Keep in mind that your worth is rooted in Jesus' finished work for you on the cross, not in your daily performance. Then you won't constantly find yourself bending over waiting to be spanked by some giant wooden spoon. You also need to learn how to love others as much as He loves you, so you will gradually move away from a preoccupation with your own selfish needs. Finally, you need to receive healing from your past experiences so you can move on to a brighter future.

Because fear is a spirit, you may also need to address fear in a spiritual manner, praying away the negative forces that are trying to distract you and keep you away from your peace and joy. There may even be times that a spirit of fear has taken such root in your life that you need the prayers of others to drive it away. Such an experience happened to me when I was a young mother. It involved the issue of snakes. I'll bet many of you can relate to that!

Of course, there is such a thing as a "healthy" fear of snakes. There are two levels of fear that we sometimes face. One type is the unnatural, pervasive sort of fear that paralyzes us and interferes with normal living. The other kind is a natural, momentary fear that can come in very handy during the course of normal life. If a copperhead were curled up in front of my door this morning when I went out to get the paper, I wouldn't be very smart if I knelt down to pet him. On the other hand, if I barricaded the house and wouldn't go out for a year, I might have a slight problem.

It's likely that many of you share my dislike of reptiles. Women and snakes don't seem to get along very well. Of course, the Bible tells us there's a reason for this, but I doubt we would have been best friends even without that experience in the Garden of Eden. When I was growing up in Milwaukee, I was very happy to know that I lived in an area that was virtually devoid of snakes. Little did I know that I was going to move to the Deep South, which is home to almost every viper known to man.

When I first moved to Mississippi as a young bride, I was absolutely terrified. Once, while I was visiting my mother back in Wisconsin, my husband called from home and told me an "amusing anecdote" that happened to him in our backyard while I was gone. He had mistaken a snake for a garden hose and had almost picked it up. "Ha, ha, ha." I laughed so hard I almost stayed in Milwaukee. I went from a fun-loving, adventurous outdoor girl who loved canoeing and hiking and camping to a city-bound recluse. Every time I went over a brown, murky, Mississippi river in a car on the interstate, I felt snakes climbing up my shorts. The one time I was forced into a boat on one of those swampy puddles that my husband mistakenly called a lake, I was so petrified that I was almost comatose. The spirit of fear had completely overpowered me, and was interfering with my ability to live my life fully.

One day, I was watching the "700 Club," and one of the hosts was praying and said a woman was being delivered from a fear of snakes. I said to myself, "Well, I might as well claim that for myself." Frankly, it was a sort of half-hearted prayer on my part, because I didn't see how I could possibly get any better. The fear was so engrained. The next time I was forced to go along on a fishing expedition, however, I suddenly realized that I could walk down to the riverbank without panicking. Naturally, I still walked carefully, looked around a lot, and made a lot of noise, but that "spirit" of fear was completely gone! I went from being comatose to being cautious.

Fear is an insidious spirit, however. Even after you think you have driven it away, it can come back in another fashion. For many years, I lived without any irrational fears in my life. Following my genuine conversion to Christianity, most of my worries about the future, including the fear of becoming a widow, began to subside. However, about a year ago, I felt the spirit of fear creeping back into my life. It started rather innocuously, while I was reading the novel, *The End of the Age*, by Pat Robertson.

This book is a fictional account of a meteor that strikes the earth and sends the world into the end-times scenario described in the Book of Revelation. Unfortunately, I have a fantastic imagination. After reading that novel, and listening to several modern-day prophets discussing end-times, I became completely convinced that the world was going to blow up by the year 2000. I became obsessed with visions of hiding in caves and subsisting on stored rations. Garbage cans full of rice and beans began to take over my basement.

Although I had always believed in family readiness, stockpiled food, tried to remain out of debt, and stressed the development of necessary skills, I had never previously thought of myself as a survivalist. Suddenly, I was gripped by an irrational fear and completely reduced to rubble. For several weeks, I couldn't function normally!

To some degree, I think this was caused by my motherly instinct. When faced with legitimate danger, it is somewhat natural for mothers to react in this manner. Despite the fact that this was hardly "legitimate danger," I found myself absolutely panicking about my children's future. At one seminar, somebody asked me why I was going to let my sixteen-year-old daughter go away to college and I actually stood there in front of hundreds of women and told them that I didn't think she would ever be able to marry and have children, and I at least wanted her to be able to have the college experience. Real great, Mary! I was using my position as a speaker to infect everyone else with my own irrational fears.

The verse that sustained me through this experience, and eventually helped me return to sanity, was the one that says, "But of that day and hour knoweth no man, nay not the angels of Heaven, but my Father only" (Matthew 24:36). Even the angels don't know when He is going to return! Why are some of these modern-day prophets so sure they know? It's true that we are seeing signs of the end of the age, but so did the disciples! They were convinced that Jesus would come back in their lifetimes. If all the people in the intervening years had simply stopped their lives in mid-stream and waited for the end to come, they would have wasted the best years of their lives waiting. I'm determined to avoid that scenario for the rest of my life. It really doesn't make any difference whether I wind up as a white-haired lady, sitting in a rocking chair knitting and watching my grandchildren out in the yard, or whether I'm taken to Heaven next week. The important thing is that I know I'm ready whenever Jesus does come back to earth, and that I do what I can to get other people ready, too.

The real reason for most fear in the world is the underlying fear of death. Even my fear of the apocalypse coming in my lifetime was really rooted in this fear. Christians shouldn't be afraid of death, because Jesus has promised us that He will give us everlasting life. I really believe that. The problem is, I'm afraid I won't like it. To be honest, Heaven has always sounded awfully dull to me. I have no desire to stand someplace, even if it is right smack next to Jesus, holding up my hands and praising Him for all eternity. B-O-R-I-N-G. Sorry if that sounds irreverent, but Jesus wants truth, and that is truth for me. Also, this whole idea of jewels and rubies and rivers of glass doesn't do much for me. I'm a grass and trees and horses kind of person. I don't even wear jewelry, so the idea of rubies and emeralds leaves me kind of cold. I've really struggled with this issue over the years. Frankly, I'm not sure I want to live forever if it's in a city made of glass and jewels, where I'm going to be bored silly for a zillion years. On top of that, the Bible says we won't be married any more! I used to think that meant I wouldn't have my family around, and that sure didn't make the scene any more appealing to me.

However, the Bible assures us that, in Heaven, He will wipe away the tears from our eyes. That means He is going to eliminate the source of those tears, not simply hand us a handkerchief! On a practical level, that means that one of two things is going to have to happen. Either I will be changed in some manner, so that I will absolutely adore standing in one place with my hands raised for a zillion years, or I will simply have a different assignment. Jesus told us that there are many mansions in Heaven. I doubt He meant that literally. He probably meant that there were many different types of places, and different assignments, each one based on our individual needs and preferences. He also mentioned something about making some of us rulers along with Him someday. Now, that has serious possibilities!

The bottom line, once again, is simply this: Do I really believe that my Heavenly Father loves me? Do I think He understands and appreciates my needs? If so, He will not put me in a place where I will be bored and unhappy and leave me there for all eternity. As long as I remain here on earth, He will never leave me comfortless (John 14:18). Although I may go through occasional trials and griefs, and "weeping may endure for a night," the joy will always return "in the morning" (Ps. 30:5). If I really believe these things, I will stop fearing the future. That's the only way I will ever be able to concentrate on the present and learn to live an abundant life in the fullness of His joy. Your need is the same as mine. If you are going through a phase where you fear the future, search for His love. Once you truly discover it, you will never have reason to be fearful again.

Chapter Four

Trusting God with the Present

"This is the day that the Lord hath made, we will rejoice and be glad in it." (Psalm 118:24)

Many people fail to live abundantly in the present, despite God's clear promise, "I am come that they might have life, and that they might have it more abundantly" (John 10:10). These people are too hung up thinking about their past or worrying about their future to enjoy the time they have now to spend with their friends and loved ones.

It might sound like a cliché, but the present is all we have. There will always be a past to think about. We will always have a future to dream about. However, the only time we have to enjoy, to do anything meaningful, or to make any necessary changes, is the time that is before us this minute, this hour.

Many home-schooling mothers allow their present to be stolen away by the demon of "busy-ness." They go through life trying desperately to feel like they have adequately accomplished everything they set out to do. The problem is, there are never enough hours in the day to accomplish their goals. There is always another toilet to be cleaned, another lesson plan to be worked up, another supper to be put on the table, another paper to be corrected, another meeting to attend, another church service to prepare for, another day of library trips and grocery shopping and trips to the post office and the bank.

No wonder these mothers are stressed out! They are so busy being busy that their lives have become barren. Their joy left them long ago, because they have become so concerned about meeting the needs of those around them that they have forgotten to enjoy the time they spend with their loved ones. They have forgotten that they have needs of their own that must be met. They have forgotten the special joy that comes from time spent quietly with the Lord. Instead, Bible study has become one more item to check off on a duty sheet before flopping into bed for a few hours sleep and starting over again the next day.

Much of this busy-ness has been self-imposed. As home-schooling mothers, we have been assigned certain responsibilities. However, we were never given the responsibility for teaching our children everything they will ever need to know. We were never asked to keep our houses looking like "Better Homes and Gardens" showcases. We were never given the responsibility of turning out children who are satisfactory "products." None of us was assigned the ultimate responsibility for the thoughts and actions of other people, even those of our own children or husbands.

If you believe that you are responsible for any of these things, you have assumed a yoke that is too difficult. You are trying to meet needs that you were never expected to fill. Back off and let Jesus take that yoke from you and replace it with His yoke, instead. Ask Him to point out to you the areas where you really do have responsibility. The assignments He gives you will never be too difficult for you to bear, for His yoke is "easy," and His burden is "light" (Matthew 11:30).

One of the most difficult lessons I've had to learn was how to slow down and focus on the present. I didn't fully understand the importance of this until my oldest son went off to college. Suddenly, my perspective changed. I looked at my other children and realized that they would not be with me forever. Now I look at six-year-old Steve and realize that nothing I have to do is more important than spending time with him. Of course, I have known this from an intellectual standpoint for a long time, but I never really comprehended it until I felt the first twinges of the "empty nest syndrome." Realizing what I had lost helped me to appreciate what remained. Since then, I have finally found the true contentment that had eluded me for so long. I have learned to live in the present, because the present is all I will ever have. The following poem says this far better than I can:

I AM

I was regretting the past
And fearing the future...
Suddenly, my Lord was speaking:

"My name is 'I am.'" He paused.
I waited. He continued.

"When you live in the past, with its mistakes
and regrets, it is hard. I am not there.
My name is not 'I was.'

When you live in the future, with fears, it is hard,
I am not there.
My name is not 'I will be.'

When you live in this moment, it is not hard.
I am here.
My name is 'I AM.'"

Anonymous

"Godliness with contentment is great gain."
(I Tim 6:6)

Chapter Five

Learning to Be Content

In Philippians 4:11, we read, "I have learned, in whatsoever state I am, therewith to be content." Of course, I know that Paul was referring to a state of mind (or a condition of wealth or want) when he wrote that, but at one point in my life, I was absolutely convinced he was talking about the State of Mississippi.

When I first met my husband, I was living in Madison, Wisconsin, surrounded by friends and interesting activities. I was an active member of a popular bluegrass band. We were having a blast. I lived an hour away from my mother and brothers, so anytime I wanted to see my family, I could hop on the bus and be there before nightfall. I had a good job, a nice apartment, lots of friends, an interesting, exciting life, and even a measure of fame. I also had a handsome, dashing sweetheart, who drifted in and out of my life just often enough to keep the fire lit. Yet, with all of this going for me, something was missing.

One day, I remember walking down a country lane and praying, "God, I'm ready to settle down. If I'm not with the right person, please send me the man you want me to be with." Just two months later, Roy came into my life. I can't say it was love at first sight, but from the minute I laid eyes on him, I knew he was the man God had sent. At first, it appeared to be useless to try to "hook" him, since he lived in Mississippi and was returning the next day, but I kept repeating God's promise, "Nothing shall be impossible unto you" (Matt. 17:20). By the following fall, I had moved to Mississippi and we were engaged. I believed that I was finally going to be totally happy, fulfilled, and living in God's will, but I hadn't counted on how lost and alone I'd feel living so far away from my former life.

For several years, the flame of young love was strong enough to weather the occasional bouts of depression and loneliness. I was happy with my marriage, happy with our new house, and happy taking care of my little babies. Then the "seven-year-itch" caught up with me in force. Suddenly, I began entertaining thoughts of leaving. "If only Roy wasn't around," I thought, "I could go back home today." Still, I knew that I was committed to a Christian marriage. No matter how much I missed what I thought of as home and family, I knew there was no way I could ever really leave. I felt like a prisoner, trapped in chains that I had donned voluntarily. The situation worsened when my older brother got married. We managed to go back home for the ceremony, but were only able to stay one day due to an approaching winter storm. Back in the Southland, I was so lonesome for my family that I thought I was going to explode. I kept trying to repeat that verse from Philippians. "Content ... content in the state I am ... content in Mississippi ... content away from my family..." But I just couldn't find any peace.

One afternoon in the bathroom, I sank to my knees in despair. (As you know, when you have young children, the bathroom is always the preferred place for totally losing it.) I was completely out of control, and sat sobbing, completely hysterical. I couldn't stand it anymore. I felt like the desire to be with my family in Wisconsin, coupled with my inability to move away from my family in Mississippi, was going to cause me to explode. I screamed out, "God, DO SOMETHING!"

That very evening, I was sitting up in bed watching television, eating a bowl of chocolate-covered ice cream that could have easily fed an entire army. (Consolation comes in many forms.) Whether it was the quadruple dose of chocolate, or delayed stress from the bathroom experience, or simply God's plan to teach me a lesson, I suddenly began to feel really weird. Within a matter of minutes, my heart began to flutter and quit working properly. We quickly called over our neighbors to watch the children, and headed for the hospital. I will never forget the feeling that came over me as I left three-year-old Sam and baby Ginny. I knew there was a distinct possibility that I was dying, and would never see them again. I lay curled up on the front seat and begged God to let me come back home to them. Never once did I say, "Please God, let me live so I can go see my mother and my brothers." Suddenly, I knew who my real family was.

That night, in the hospital, I lay on the cold, metal examining table. I was dimly aware of the doctor asking me a million questions that I was incapable of answering. I heard Roy answering the questions, and could tell how worried he was. Yet, somehow, I felt totally detached from the situation. I felt sorry for Roy, but it was as if he existed in one dimension, and I had temporarily stepped into another one. There was another man standing, just off to my left. I couldn't see Him clearly. I could just make out His form. He didn't speak, but I knew exactly who He was, and what He was doing there. He was there to let me know He was in charge, and everything was going to be okay, and it was.

The doctor eventually diagnosed, "mitral valve prolapse" as the cause of my problem, and told me this would probably haunt me all my life. He tried hard to put me on medicine, but I wouldn't do it because I was still nursing a baby. He told me that once the baby was weaned, it was imperative that I go on the medicine, and it would be best never to have any more children, since having another episode while pregnant or nursing could cause a major problem.

That was sixteen years and three children ago. I have had a few more episodes of "atrial fibrillation" since then, which means the upper part of the heart goes nuts and forgets what it is supposed to be doing. In each case, I have taken an aspirin (to prevent clotting) and gone to bed for a day or so, reciting Bible verses. I have never had to return to the hospital or go on the medication the doctor ordered.

But the biggest lesson this whole experience taught me concerned contentment. When the chips were down, and I thought I was a goner, I didn't think about my old family, I thought about my new family. When I needed Him, the Lord was there. I learned that He is the source of my contentment, and I never need to look any further to get myself out of a state of confusion or despair.

Does this mean I am always 100% content nowadays? Of course not. Right now, I long to live in the country. I want a pasture full of horses and a barnyard full of chickens and a huge garden and a cornfield. I want ten acres of woods to wander through in the late afternoon, after the chores are done. I've wanted all of this since I was ten years old, and have hardly ever stepped foot out of my semi-boring suburban existence. Over the years I've learned, however, that if God really wanted me to live in the country at this point in my life, I'd already be there. Since I'm not there yet, I must be where I should be now. If He doesn't want me to live in the country right now, and I were to force it, I'd be out of His will, and therefore miserable despite my surroundings.

Someday, I believe that it will be His will for us to make that move, but until then I have truly learned to be content in whatever state (condition) I am. After all, where I am is where I am, no matter what I may think about it. That means I have two basic choices. I can either stay here grumbling and wishing I was elsewhere, and missing all that's special about this part of my life, or I can wait patiently, enjoying my time with my family and hoping for a future that is even brighter. I've learned to choose the latter.

I've learned one other thing from this entire experience, too. From now on, I play to pray a little more specifically.

"The bush burned with fire, and the bush was not consumed."
(Exodus 3:2)

Chapter Six

Burned Out vs. On Fire

A short time ago, a young mother called and asked if she could come over for some counseling. When she arrived at the door, she had four small children in tow. I could immediately sense that she was tense and distraught. We sat down and tried to have a conversation, but it was constantly punctuated with disciplinary threats directed at the two boys:

"R ---, I'm trying to have a conversation with Mrs. Hood."

"J---, leave your sister's pigtails alone."

When I suggested that the children might be happier playing outside, the mother told me she would prefer that they stay right where they were. She didn't trust them going outside alone. I indicated that my sixteen-year-old daughter would be happy to watch them for a few minutes, but she said that they didn't "do well" with outsiders. So we continued to talk while the boys tumbled around the living room, and the girls hung onto her skirts. She was never able to finish a single sentence, or listen to my sage advice, because the children occupied her attention the entire time she was there.

Finally, I broke through a little bit. "Why did you come here today?" I asked. "I just needed to talk to someone older than eight!" she sighed. "I'm so burned out with the constant responsibility of four young children. I never get anything done. I never have any time for myself."

This mother was mistaking her legitimate parental responsibilities for martyrdom. She was trying to control every movement that her children made. She didn't trust the children outside, despite having a fenced yard and a sliding glass door through which we could watch them. She didn't trust my daughter to watch the children. She didn't trust the children to behave themselves out of her sight. She wasn't able to finish a single sentence because she was so worried that the children might somehow offend me and make me think she wasn't a good mother. In short, she didn't trust God to take care of her children without her constant meddling. No wonder she characterized herself as a "burned-out homeschooling mom." She had set a pace for herself that was virtually impossible to continue.

I'd like to contrast that homeschooling mother with another one I've known for many years. This woman has seven children. Her children are not perfect. Her house is not immaculate. Her family has never been featured on the cover of a home-schooling magazine. She has had troubles and griefs over the years, but she always maintains a peaceful presence. She is perfectly capable of carrying on an adult conversation over the occasional din of children and pets. What makes the difference? She recognizes that she is not the one who is really in control. She has let go and let God take care of her family, and therefore can stay tranquil and joyful in the midst of occasional turbulence.

I read about a contest at an art show once. The judges were asked to choose the painting that best depicted "tranquility." Most patrons imagined that the winner might be a picture of an idyllic tropical island, a placid sea, a field of flowers, or possibly a Madonna and child gazing tenderly into each other's eyes. The painting that won was actually a portrayal of a violent storm. The thunder was crashing and the winds roaring. Right in the middle of the storm was a mother bird, sitting on a nest, calmly holding her wings over her babies and resting.

Now that is a picture of true serenity. That mother has everything together, precisely because she is not trying to control anything. She is trusting that God has control of the storm, and she is concentrating on doing her own job, barely even aware of the wind and the rain.

God is our source of constant energy. When we are plugged into His power source, we can get charged up and remain "on fire" indefinitely, burning with his love, working endlessly for His kingdom. Those people who get burned out are allowing something to block this flow of energy from God. Sometimes it is worry or fear. Sometimes it is a lack of sufficient obedience to the still voice of God inside. Sometimes it is a lack of trust in other people, or a lack of trust in God. Sometimes it is a yoke that they have voluntarily taken which has proven too heavy to bear. When God is truly in control, there is no burnout. When Moses saw the burning bush, "he looked and behold, the bush burned with fire, and the bush was not consumed." Moses wondered what was going on, and said to himself, "I will draw aside and see ... why the bush is not burnt." The answer, of course, is that God was in the center of the burning bush. His presence is an Almighty Fire that can never be consumed (Exodus, 3,4).

God is still with us today. He is our source of power and our strength. He is our peace and our tranquility. When we stop trying to control the storms of life, when we concentrate instead on those responsibilities that are legitimately ours, burnout ceases to be a problem. The problem arises when we resist the flow of His power, and try to interfere or take on jobs that we have not been asked to perform.

Consider a light bulb for a moment. Do you know how a light bulb works? Or any electrical appliance? (If not, consider a unit study on electricity!) A light bulb is plugged into a wall socket, and energy races through the wires. Electricity can run along well-kept wires for years without ever producing heat. The reason a light bulb glows (and eventually burns out) lies in the fact that it is providing resistance. The filament heats up, temporarily blocking the flow of power. Eventually, this increased heat will cause it to self-destruct.

Hudson Taylor, the great missionary to China, once mused about what would happen if just one person were ever able to completely eliminate his resistance to God. Just think what God could do with a person like that! Such a person could literally change the world! In fact, that's exactly what Christ did. He was the only person who was ever completely molded to His Father's will, and He did change the world, forever! He never burned out, because He was perfectly yielded to His Father's will, perfectly focused, and perfectly at peace. (And remember, He promised that the things He did, we can do also, if we just believe in Him! (John 14:12))

Instead of allowing ourselves to become "burned out,' we need to learn how to stay on fire, like the burning bush. Each morning we should arise, eager to do and be everything the Lord has commanded us. We should try to be totally without resistance, totally without an agenda of our own. This doesn't mean we should never have goals or plans. It just means that we should never let those plans get in the way of listening to the still, small voice of God inside.

I'd like to close this section with two word pictures that may help some of you learn to stay connected to your power source. The Bible says, "Thou wilt keep him in perfect peace, whose mind is stayed on thee" (Isaiah 26:3). A sailing ship has one large main mast, right in the center. All of the other parts of the ship are stabilized by being fastened or "stayed" to this mast. If the lines are ever severed, the boat may founder. Jesus spent a lot of time on boats. Several of his disciples were fishermen by trade. The Bible used this example to remind us that He is our main mast. When we "stay" our lives to His life, attaching ourselves firmly to the sturdy center pole, our ship will never sink, although it may sometimes be tossed by raging seas.

The second example is for you gardeners out there. In the fifteenth chapter of John, Jesus gives His own recipe for reclaiming joy when it appears to be missing. In this chapter, He says:

"Abide in me, and I in you. As the branch cannot bear fruit of itself, except it abide in the vine, no more can ye, except ye abide in me. I am the vine, ye are the branches. He that abideth in me, and I in Him, the same bringeth forth much fruit, for without me, ye can do nothing.

If a man abide not in me, he is cast forth as a branch, and is withered, and men gather them, and cast them into the fire, and they are burned. If ye abide in me, and my words abide in you, ye shall ask what ye will, and it shall be done unto you. Herein is my Father glorified, that ye bear much fruit; so shall ye be my disciples. As the father hath loved me, so have I loved you. Continue ye in my love. If ye keep my commandments, ye shall abide in my love, even as I have kept my Father's commandments, and abide in His love.

...These things have I spoken unto you, that my joy might remain in you, and that your joy might be full."
(John 15:4-11).

Part Two:

Homeschooling With Joy

"Be still, and know that I am God."
(Ps. 46:10)

"Seek and ye shall find..."
(Matt 7:7)

Chapter Seven

The Search for the Right Questions

I receive phone calls and letters every day from people who are either interested in homeschooling their children, or are having difficulty getting on track with their homeschooling efforts. You've probably already heard most of the questions they ask. "How can I know what grade level my child is on?" How can I teach five children who are all on different grade levels?" How can I teach my high schooler if I don't know algebra?" How can I have time to home school my children and still do my housework and have some personal time?", and of course, the ever popular, "But what about socialization?"

These questions are difficult to answer for a single reason. People are asking the wrong questions! It is hard to come up with satisfactory answers when the questions themselves are steeped in error.

Most of these questions are based on a view of the home school as a tiny institutional school, complete with grade levels, lesson plans, tests, and grades. We do not have such a school in our household. I'm a mother. I am not a teacher who stands at the front of a classroom. My husband is not the principal of a school. He is a husband and father and the head of our little household. I'm convinced that God never called any of us to set up miniature institutions for our children. He wants us to go back to His original plan for the family, and be the best parents we can be. That is totally sufficient.

Children are not cattle. They were never meant to be raised in herds. The entire concept of the institutional school was man-made. God did not create schools. He placed us in families, and gave us fairly simple directions. We were given some instructions regarding discipline and proper relationships. We were also given the responsibility of teaching our children about God and His Word. Period. The Bible never makes mention of lesson plans, tests, or curriculum choices. There are no grade levels mentioned, and no lists of required subjects. These are all concepts that were created by educators who needed to develop methods for working with large groups of children in an institutional setting.

The institutional school did not even exist for most children until the mid 1800s. The movement that created the public schools was based on a secular mindset. Although the smaller schools often used Christian materials back in the 1800s, the founders of the public school movement in America were primarily men like Horace Mann, who deliberately set out to establish schools that would undermine the religious beliefs of "closed-minded" parents.

As institutional schools took root in America, parents gradually began to turn more and more of their God-given responsibilities over to the state. Eventually, the state had an almost complete monopoly on the education of the young. The next step was centralization. Local control gradually eroded. Although the Constitution clearly did not intend federal involvement in education, we now have a federal "Department of Education," which is trying its best to create federal goals and the standardization of curricula across the board. Most of you are already familiar with such trends as "Goals 2000," "Outcomes-Based Education," and national testing programs. What you may not realize is that such ideas have been around since the very conception of the public education system in the mid-1800s. They are simply more prominent now than they were then, and the stage has been set for their implementation now that God has been kicked out of the decision-making process.

I really don't believe God ever liked the idea of institutional education, but He allowed it to flourish as long as most schools were still teaching the Bible and focusing on character education. God's best scenario was the one He gave us to begin with: a circle of parents and children, working, learning, and growing together. His next best scenario, the one He tolerated for many years in America, was a small group of children being taught God's Word for short periods of time away from their families. Gradually small groups became large groups; short periods of time gave way to marathon sessions where the children were separated from their parents all day every day. Finally His Word was banished from the classroom. At that point, He shouted, "ENOUGH!" Since then, public education has consistently slid downhill.

The Bible says, "Without me, you can do NOTHING" (John 15:5). All the reforms, and the funding increases, and the "magnet schools," and the "charter schools" have one important thing in common. They are all doomed to failure. It says so right in the Bible. Without Him, nothing of redeeming value can ever be accomplished. Of course, there are still individual teachers and principals who are Christians and who are trying their best to bring Him back into their individual classrooms. These people are the salt and light still found in the system, and do not necessarily share the same fate as the system itself. On a small scale, these trained, mature Christian soldiers can accomplish a great deal. However, on a large scale, the entire setup is doomed to failure unless there is massive repentance and true reform. (Notice I'm talking about adults when I'm talking about "salt and light" within the school system. Any general knows that you don't put immature, untrained soldiers in the middle of a raging war and expect them to be conquering heroes. Young children are much more likely to be influenced by the negative forces around them than to provide "salt and light" for their classmates. If such children have to be in the public system, the *parents* must be the ones who are praying for their safety, watching carefully for the negative influences, and impacting the system with their Christian witness.)

When God finally said, "Enough!", the modern-day homeschooling movement began in earnest. One by one, individual parents began to feel nudges in this direction. We were among those early homeschoolers. Fourteen years ago, our oldest son was just about to enter first grade in a public school. The Sunday before he was supposed to start, an article appeared in the newspaper about homeschooling, and gave us the answer for which we had been searching. I'm sure it was no coincidence.

Like many other parents, we began the process without knowing the first thing about homeschooling. Naturally, we based our early efforts on what we already knew about education. Lesson plans. Textbooks. Workbooks. Grades. Chalkboard at the front. Learning and life were separated into neat little compartments and parceled out in pre-digested mouthfuls. It didn't take long to find out that this arrangement didn't work for our family. I could actually see the love of learning being extinguished in our children's eyes.

That clearly wasn't what God had in mind for our family. Like many parents, we had simply misunderstood what He had called us to do. He didn't ask us to set up a tiny institutional school in our home. He asked us to refrain from putting our impressionable little sponges into a Godless group environment for the major part of the day. He called us back to His original plan for the family. He wanted us to live and work and learn and play and pray together. Above all, He called us back to our original responsibility:

> *"These words, which I command thee this day, shall be in thine heart, and thou shalt teach them diligently unto thy children and shalt talk of them*

*when thou sittest in thine house, and when thou
walkest by the way, and when thou liest down, and
when thou riseth up" (Deut 6:6-7).*

We certainly couldn't have lived up to that
commandment if our children were away from us all day
long five days a week, during their most receptive hours. In
order to be obedient to God's command for our family, we
had to learn to become students ourselves, so that we could
figure out what He really had in mind for us. We had to
develop enough trust in Him to believe that He would direct
our paths, and that He cared enough about our
homeschooling efforts to help us with the smallest details of
everyday life at home.

As we gradually discovered that God's plan for our
family was not synonymous with our own beliefs about
education, we had to turn to Him to find the wisdom needed
to properly train our children in His way. That took a lot of
thought, since we had many assumptions about education
that we were carrying around as excess baggage from our
own days in public school. I'm sure you have a lot of
preconceived ideas about education, too. Before we can
begin to find the right questions to ask about Godly
homeschooling, we have to identify and eliminate some of
these old secular assumptions, so we can start from scratch.

You know the type of assumptions I'm talking about:
the need for tests, grades, grade levels and lesson plans; for
teaching eight subjects to a group of thirty students at a time
for seven periods a day with the teacher up at the board and
the students sitting quietly in place at their desks. Then there
is all the educational paraphernalia: chalkboards, teacher's
desks, globes and flags at the front of the classroom. We've
even appropriated the apple on the teacher's desk and used it
as a symbol of homeschooling. Of course, there is nothing
inherently wrong with taking some of the methods,
materials, or symbols we associate with institutional

education and adapting them to suit our purposes. However, we cannot just take an institutional model and try to make it fit the homeschooling situation. It simply doesn't work. We each need to think through our assumptions, eliminating any that don't seem appropriate anymore, and construct a new model, one that is tailor-made for our individual families.

When God made us into "new creatures" (II Cor 5:17), He didn't leave all our old habits and mindsets in place, did He? He started fresh, with a clean slate. That's what we need to do, too. In the next chapter, we are going to think through some old assumptions about education, and discuss the need for creating new structures. These structures may look different from one family to another. God never intended for us to be clones of each other. Your ideas about education may be very different from mine. That's not important. What is important is that you seek your own guidance and make conscious decisions about what is right for your own family.

Wipe your slate clean today. Lose all your old, outmoded ideas about what a "school" should look like, and start over with a fresh outlook. Think about what "education" is really all about. Develop new questions that are based on the home and the family, rather than a miniature institution. With the proper questions in place, you will finally be able to find the answers that will work for your family!

Chapter Eight

New Wineskins for New Wine

"Neither do men put new wine into old bottles, else the bottles break, and the wine runneth out, and the bottles perish; but they put new wine into new bottles, and both are preserved." (Matt 9:17

In order to create new structures for our families, we must first get rid of the old ones. The Bible states that it is foolish to place new wines into old wineskins, because the old wineskins will burst under the strain (Matt 9:17). The "old wineskins" of institutional education are not going to properly contain your homeschooling efforts. Without new structures, your efforts will collapse under the strain of trying to fit into an inadequate mold.

When you made the decision to become homeschoolers, you started out with one major disadvantage. You already knew too much about education! If you were beginning an enterprise with zero experience, you would realize you had to start from scratch. Since you had spent at least twelve years in an institutional setting, you were starting out with a lot of excess baggage. You had a ton of assumptions you were carrying around with you regarding the nature of teaching and learning. For most of you, such assumptions were formed in a secular, group setting. Now that God has called you to teach your children as individuals in a Christian setting, many of those beliefs you have formed about education are not going to be valid anymore, and you are going to have to come up with new ones.

There are hundreds of assumptions about learning and education that you are already carrying around inside your head. You need to gradually identify some of them and decide consciously which ones are still workable and true, and which ones need to be changed. We will discuss some of the more prevalent ones here, but you need to be constantly alert to others that surface. You must learn to challenge every idea that presents itself to you and ask questions like, "Why do I believe this?", "Where did this idea come from?", "Does it make sense anymore?", "Is this what God really wants for our family?"

Let's begin with the concept of "grade level." People are always asking me questions such as, "How do I know what grade level my child is on in reading?", and "Is it okay if my child is two grade levels higher in science than in social studies?" Others worry, "My child is behind his grade level in math. Should I be concerned about the authorities getting after me? What will happen if he has to go back to school someday? How will he fit in?"

These people are treating the concept of "grade level" as if it was the law of gravity! Just remember, somebody thought up the idea of grade levels to begin with. Grade levels were created by teachers who were faced with thirty new students at the beginning of every school year. These teachers had to have some way to decide what was typically taught in the third grade, and how to identify those in need of remedial attention or extra challenges. You don't have thirty new children a year. Why should you be worried about your child's grade level? Do you really want to use the standard of the public school system as your measuring stick?

For home-schooling parents, the important thing is to seek God's will for your children, and set some worthwhile goals for them. Next, you need to assess their current ability levels and begin working from there. If the authorities ever criticize your efforts, explain your goals and your children's needs and how you are addressing them. Professional educators understand that all students don't learn at the same pace. If they were going to put teachers out of business whenever they had slow children in their classrooms, the schools would be shut down within a week. If one of your children appears to be below "grade level," remind them of that and stand your ground! Also remember that slow doesn't mean stupid. Turtles are slow because God made them that way. So are some kids. So are some parents and educators, for that matter!

If your children do have to go back to a school setting some day, the teachers have been trained to identify needs and design programs to meet those needs. Let them do their jobs when and if it becomes necessary. You concentrate on doing your job in the present without worrying about the future. Besides, I think that those of us who have been called to homeschool our children should start treating it as if it were a commitment, and not constantly worry about what will happen "if they go back to school." If God wants them at home with you, He will make sure they can stay there indefinitely. If it is His will that they return someday, He can take care of that situation, too!

Another concept that needs to be challenged concerns the organization of the curriculum. In school, the teachers are expected to cover several subjects at the same time. Reading, language arts, math, social studies, and science are usually required in the elementary grades. Some systems add in extras, like art, music, foreign languages, computers, and physical education. Stop and think for just a moment about the way we learn as adults. I certainly don't say to myself, "What eight areas should I work on this week?" Rather, I tend to focus on one area at a time. Sometimes, if I'm really motivated, I may have two or three areas of concentration. This year, for example, I want to write this book, and also hope to get back in good physical condition. I'm also piddling around a little with learning Russian. I certainly don't have eight curriculum areas I'm working on at once in my own life. Why should I expect my students to spread themselves that thin? What would it prove?

When allowed to learn in a more natural fashion, children also tend to focus on one or two things at a time. When Dan, my thirteen-year-old son, was about six, he went on a math binge for about two months. During that time, he ate, slept, and did math. In two months, he completed an entire year's worth of work. Then he didn't do any math at all for about a year and a half. When he started up again, it took him only about a week to remember what he had done, and then he took off again in earnest. Another time, he spent an entire year studying social studies. He got the maps and the globe and put them in his bedroom. He read two history textbooks and numerous biographies. He poured over maps and memorized the names of countries, capitol cities, and geographical features. During that year, he didn't do any other subjects at all (in an academic fashion), but he learned enough about history and geography to beat all the adults on "Jeopardy" every night.

During that time, I also managed to create enough records to satisfy the authorities that instruction was taking place in other areas of the curriculum. Did I report that no math took place? Of course not. We used math at my curriculum table, in the grocery store, and in the kitchen that year. Did I say we didn't do any science? We went for walks in the woods, visited the zoo, and started an aquarium. We didn't have to "hit the books" in every subject to find enough things to report on an evaluation form. (We'll talk more about this subject in a later chapter. I also have written a booklet, entitled, "Relaxed Record Keeping", in case you want details.)

The point, however, is not that I have an intelligent child who was interested in social studies one year. The point is not that I have worked out a system for reporting relaxed learning experiences, either. The point is that when he went off on this particular tangent, I didn't step in and interfere with his learning. I didn't automatically insist that he spend equal amounts of time in all areas of the curriculum just because some manual or sheet of paper provided by the county board of education said I should. That assumption needed to be challenged and broken in order to make the most of his natural desire to delve deeply into one area at a time. You need to challenge such assumptions, too. Listen to that little voice inside of you that lets you know when something is working, and when something is in need of change. Whether it is the Holy Spirit speaking to you, or simply your mother's intuition, you can figure out how to deal with any situation, if you just take the time to think things over carefully.

Another widely held assumption involves the need to "cover" certain subjects in order to turn out a well-rounded adult. Personally, I don't care if my children ever "cover" anything! I covered every subject known to man on my quest for two master's degrees and a Ph.D., and got A's in all of them. I took every "-ology" that has ever been created. If you asked me to stand up and give you a five-minute lecture on any one of them, I couldn't do it! You see, I learned how to play a game called "college." I took a zillion subjects, one by one, learning just enough to spit out a few answers on a test. The instructor said, "There. Now she knows all about this subject." WRONG. What I actually accomplished was getting my "A," sticking my three credits into my portfolio, and moving on. I did that subject after subject, wasting years and years without ever learning what "true education" meant. Covering information, by itself, does not ensure that any true, lasting learning takes place.

A corollary to these assumptions is the supposed requirement to plan instruction in advance and purchase $300 worth of curriculum materials each year in order for education to be meaningful. I have never made out a lesson plan in my life. The curriculum materials I purchase at the start of each school year have dwindled to practically nothing. Has this lack of advanced planning and purchasing hampered learning? My sixteen-year-old daughter just received a high SAT score, enabling her to win an honor's scholarship to her first-choice college. Somebody must have thought she learned enough along the way to be adequately prepared for college!

Who's In Charge Here, Anyway?

The process of identifying and rooting out assumptions is one of the first steps in taking control of your children's education. Most of you became homeschoolers because you wanted to have that control. However, the first thing many of you do is give control away again. You give it away to curriculum publishers, textbook authors, mothers-in-law, or home-schooling friends. You give it away when you buy a $300 curriculum package because one person said it worked for them. You give it away when you feel compelled to use and "finish" the $300 curriculum package long after you realize that it isn't working for your particular children. You give it away when you get so scared of the authorities that you feel like you have to tailor your curriculum to their goals instead of your own. Husbands sometimes give it away to wives, and wives to their husbands. In order to really take control, you must all think for yourselves, and then communicate effectively with your spouses so you can act together as a team.

So go ahead! Take back control of your homeschooling efforts and create a "new wineskin" that is tailor-made for your own family. Throw the old, outdated structures away. Challenge every assumption that comes along. Find the right questions to ask, and begin your search for the proper answers for your particular situation. Just don't forget the most important step of all! Once you have taken back control from those who have tried to seize it from you, you must give it away one more time. Your home school will never be truly successful, relaxed, or joyful until you have stopped trying to control and manage everything yourself, and turned that responsibility back over to God.

"Of making many books there is no end, and much study is a weariness of the flesh." (Ecc. 12:12)

Chapter Nine

Real, Enthusiastic Learning

The year was 1990. I had just completed thirty-five years of structured education, possibly setting a new record for being a perpetual student. After twelve years in the public school, one bachelor's degree, two master's degrees, and a Ph.D., I was totally burned out on education. I felt like I never wanted to read a book again in my life. My motivation for learning new subjects was completely gone.

Despite this lack of motivation, I was faced with a major dilemma. As a homeschooling mother, I knew I needed to get excited about learning again myself if I ever expected my children to love to read and learn new things. Eventually, I did get my own motivation back, but it took me about a year of "down time" to become rejuvenated and develop enthusiasm for learning again.

If you are lucky enough to be motivated already, you are truly blessed. However, if your own motivation level is low, you can get it back just like I did. If your children were already in an institutional school, they may also have lost their motivation for learning, but they will eventually become rejuvenated if you are willing to back off a little bit and give them some space, too.

I vividly remember the day, about one year after my Ph.D. program ended, when I was walking through the library with my children and got the urge to take out a novel for myself. I almost cried. It was as if something that had once been very important to me had suddenly been given back as a gift. I realized how much I had missed as a result of being exposed to thirty-five years of teacher-directed structure that had completely eroded my own motivation for learning.

As I mentioned in the last chapter, I don't believe that true, lasting learning takes place in an atmosphere of teacher-directed coercion. There is very little of value that I remember from my college education. When students are expected to study subjects that are of no immediate interest to them, especially in a disconnected, textbook-driven manner, they will usually retain just enough in their short-term memory cells to convince the teacher that they have completed the required assignments. The information itself will go in one ear and out the other and will never be incorporated into their real lives outside of school. This phenomenon is not confined to institutional forms of education, either. It can happen in your own home if you try too hard to mimic institutional methods of artificial motivation and coercion. These methods obviously have not been working for the institutional schools. They aren't going to produce lasting benefits in your home environment, either.

There are many ways that teachers kill off motivation in their students. They do it when they don't allow the children to go off on tangents when they are truly motivated to learn about a particular subject. They do it by chopping up books and dissecting them; by turning interests into required assignments; by focusing on disconnected skills rather than the larger picture; by treating students as if they were clones of each other, growing and learning on the same timetables and with the same learning styles. After the flames of enthusiasm have been blown out, the teachers then step in with all their "external" motivators: grades, stickers, happy faces, frowny faces, pizza parties, summer reading programs at the library, and trips to amusement parks. Such motivators have one thing in common. They are all designed to convince the students subconsciously that reading and learning are things they would never do unless they were coerced.

At some point in the students' careers, they will become teenagers, too old for stickers and happy faces. By that time, they will have forgotten that they ever had any other reasons for learning or growing. They will then focus simply on jumping through the hoops, earning their grades and amassing enough credits to get out of school. The emphasis will be on "getting finished" with their education, which, in their minds, will have become synonymous with "school." Real learning will have been lost in the shuffle. That's what happened to me on my quest for my Ph.D. It's why so many older high schoolers seem so lost and disconnected. Their own motivation, in many cases, was extinguished years ago, and they no longer have the carrots and sticks to keep them going. They have been treated like children for so long that they are incapable of stepping out into the adult world with any degree of motivation, other than the desire to break free of their bonds and get out on their own.

For a moment, let's contrast the typical bored, unwilling textbook-studying high school senior with my nineteen-year-old son, Sam. His knowledge of astronomy is phenomenal. Sam probably knows as much as many professional astronomers about planets, meteors, and black holes. He was never asked to learn astronomy. It was a burning obsession for him. That is the very best type of learning, the kind that will remain for an entire lifetime. It takes place when an individual wants to learn about a subject on his own motivation, simply because he loves the material. I took astronomy in college and I got an "A" in it. However, I never knew much about the universe until Sam came along. An excited learner will cause the people around him to learn, too. Such intensity is extremely contagious.

Some people are afraid that if children are primarily allowed to study what interests them, they will grow up to be one-sided, shallow individuals. I haven't found that to be the case. Over the years, my children have been excited about all of the following at different points in their lives: baseball, theatre, geography, fish, seashells, insects, astronomy, archeology, reading, writing stories, dinosaurs, embroidery, weapons, the underground railroad, horses, dogs and cats, music, art, costumes and makeup, medieval times, World War II, cooking, woodworking, electronics, and even math! That is just a small sampling of the interests we have had over the years. Every one of those subjects was studied intensely by at least one family member without any external prodding at all. In each case, the person who was excited about a subject managed to teach the rest of us a lot, whether we wanted to hear about it or not It's hard to ignore an excited learner

That is the second-best kind of learning. It occurs when the enthusiasm of one person spills over to another. When Sam was studying astronomy, he was so excited that he constantly shared his observations with other family members. He called the younger children over to the telescope to show them interesting sights, and discussed things he read about in the newspaper concerning comets, space travel, and related subjects. Due to his unbounded enthusiasm, our other children all learned a tremendous amount of information about astronomy. Never once was it turned into a school assignment, although I did seize a couple of teachable moments, and took out a couple of books on the subject for the younger children. I was very careful not to turn the entire episode into a structured learning experience, however. There was too much learning going on to risk shutting it all down by turning it into "schoolwork."

The third type of meaningful, lasting learning takes place when an individual sets a goal and becomes willing to work hard at tasks that he or she would normally disdain in order to reach that goal. My oldest daughter recently demonstrated this in action. About a year and a half ago, she took the PSAT (a test commonly taken in the tenth grade). She had already set a goal of going to college early. When she took the test, she received an extremely high verbal score, which was not surprising, since she is a voracious reader and an excellent writer. However, her math score was pitiful. It became obvious to her that if she wanted to earn a high SAT score and enter college early, she was going to have to get serious about math.

For the first time in her life, she buckled down to study advanced math on her own initiative. We purchased a fairly expensive video series from the Chalk Dust Company, because she is a visual learner and had a difficult time with a textbook approach. Every morning, she worked diligently at algebra and geometry. I never had to urge her to sit down and do her work. She was completely self-motivated, despite the fact that math has always been her least-favorite subject. When the time finally came for her to take the SAT, her math score rose dramatically. She was able to enter college at the age of sixteen, to have her GED waived, and to earn an honor's scholarship.

Suppose for a minute that I had set this goal, rather than my daughter. If I had come in and said, "Ginny, I want you to be adequately prepared for college. Start studying math a couple of hours a day," she would have done it. However, it would have been a reluctant learning situation, and the quality of the learning would have been a lot less. I would have had to prod and prompt her, and would probably have driven both of us crazy in the process. Besides, I doubt highly that the math score would have risen that dramatically if the motivation had not been her own. The learning would not have "stuck" enough to help her get the honor's scholarship she craved.

Although the student must therefore be actively involved in the educational process in order for true, lasting learning to take place, there are still many important roles for the parents to play in encouraging and facilitating such learning. We will discuss parental roles in the following chapters. Once again, it is also important that we recognize the role that God plays in this entire process. The title of this chapter is "Real, Enthusiastic Learning." The word "enthusiasm" means literally, "in God." God is an enthusiastic teacher. When He is in His place at the center of your home, enthusiastic learning will take place, provided you allow Him to be in control. There is no need for all your frantic efforts to cover every subject known to man. There is no need for hours spent planning and worrying. There is no need to purchase a professionally designed $300 curriculum package at the start of each new school year. Trust God to show you what to do and where to find the materials that you need when they are really needed. Trust yourself and your children. Trust the Holy Spirit to motivate and direct their efforts. Teach less and pray more. If you learn to back off a little and allow education to flow from life and from these three sources of motivation, you will find yourself barely able to keep up with the flurry of enthusiastic, true learning that will be taking place in your household.

Chapter Ten

Discovering Your Real Role

One of the most important steps in developing "new wineskins" for our homeschooling efforts is to consider carefully what role each member of the team is supposed to play. Many of the questions people ask concerning their roles are based on incorrect assumptions and are therefore flawed. New homeschooling mothers wonder how anyone can possibly teach five different children at the same time that are all on different grade levels. This question is based on several related assumptions. We have already discussed the issue of grade levels. The question also assumes that a homeschooling mother's role is similar in structure and function to that of a classroom teacher. It conjures up an image of a teacher standing at the front of a home-based classroom, providing instruction for five different grade levels of math, science, social studies, language arts, music, art, and physical education, all during the course of a typical six hour day. Naturally this picture scares a lot of potential homeschoolers. Such a role would be almost impossible to maintain for very long, especially when added to the normal responsibilities connected with being a wife and mother.

Similarly, the controversy over the role of the father in the home school is based on an incorrect assumption. The question, "Is the father the principal of the home school?" can't be properly answered, because a home school is first and foremost a *home*, not an institutional *school*. The role of the father is actually far more important than that of a principal, but calling the father the "principal" can set him up to feel like a failure when he is unable to fulfill that requirement on the same level as a full-time educator. It can also cause wives to adopt unfair sets of expectations, and lose respect for their husbands when they don't perform duties they were never actually meant to assume.

Once again, we must start at the beginning. Let's try hard to forget every assumption we have about institutional schools and their structure. Let's forget about principals and teachers and even students for awhile, and go back to thinking through the proper setup of the home, as outlined in God's Word.

Building a Godly Home

The Bible begins by making it clear that a man and woman are supposed to cleave together and leave their former households behind in order to set up a new entity (Mark 10:6-9). Depending on the age of the grandparents and how far away they live, this can sometimes be easier said than done. It may be very difficult to sever "the ties that bind," but this is a crucial step in establishing a Godly home. After you have started a family of your own, you are no longer required to *obey* your own parents in the manner of young children., The instruction to *honor* your parents remains all through your lifetime. However, there is a big difference between honoring grandparents and allowing them to usurp authority that no longer properly belongs to them.

In order to continue honoring your parents and in-laws, without confusing this issue with obedience, you and your husband must present a unified front to the rest of the world, including your relatives. All decisions that relate to your family need to be made as a parental unit. When grandparents do not understand or are tempted to meddle a bit too much in the education and raising of grandchildren, you need to stand up for your own beliefs. However, this does not mean that you should simply turn your backs and hope that the grandparents will disappear. You need to listen to the grandparents' concerns, reassure them that you appreciate their input and the love they are demonstrating for their grandchildren, and then turn around and make your own decisions, based on the information you have and the guidance you receive from God.

Information and guidance can come from more than one source, however. Grandparents have been around a long time. They may make a lot of sense, so listen carefully to what they have to say. Don't automatically dismiss their comments, especially if your motivation is simply to show them that you are an adult and are therefore allowed to stick your tongue out at them. However, if you and your husband already agree on your goals, disciplinary techniques, methods of instruction, or anything else that touches your family and your homeschooling efforts, it would be a mistake to change simply because an outsider (albeit a loving, caring, close, next-of-kin outsider) has a different opinion.

The second point the Bible makes about the family concerns the need for unity (Matt 12:25). This is especially important for husbands and wives. I believe that God brings people together in marriage that are often quite dissimilar, because each of them has different strengths and abilities to contribute to the family unit. Together, they can blend into a stronger whole. If they view themselves as complementary, and try to compromise on most issues, they will find that they tend to compensate for any weaknesses found in their mates. However, when the weaknesses themselves are stressed, these very dissimilarities can sometimes lead to in fighting and bickering. That type of dissension can threaten everything the family is trying to accomplish.

Many times, one parent feels led to try homeschooling, and the other has not yet been convinced of its merits. Whenever such disputes take place, it is unfair for either partner to simply push his or her will on the other without making a genuine attempt to understand the other person's point of view. If agreement is still lacking after numerous rational discussions about the topic, the fairest course is probably to compromise and agree to try homeschooling for one year, so that both partners can have the opportunity to see how homeschooling actually works in action. That's what we did in our family. My husband was somewhat opposed at the start, but agreed to give it a try for one year. It didn't take long for him to become an enthusiastic homeschooler.

However, if the father and mother still disagree after much discussion and a trial run, I personally don't recommend continuing to teach the children at home, especially if the mother is trying to push the issue over the objections of the father. The unity of the family and the leadership of the father are more important issues than the specific method of education chosen. If God truly wants a particular family to become homeschoolers, He is perfectly capable of changing people's minds on His own. This is another situation where a little judicious "backing off" combined with a lot of prayer may be more helpful than hours of discussion and argument.

For those who make it past this hurdle, and decide to try homeschooling, it is important that the father and mother be molded into a unified team. In *The Relaxed Home School*, I used a metaphor of a theatrical production team to explain my own view of the family. In this scenario, the father is the "producer" and the mother the "director." They must agree about some basic points in order for the production to stay on track. Although the mother must be given a degree of autonomy in order for the family to function well in the father's absence, there are certain items that should be worked out together, with both team leaders involved. Both parents must be included when establishing such things as disciplinary standards and methods, general long-range goals for the family, and decisions concerning the specific roles each will play. They also need to set up special times for getting together in order to pray for family members on a regular basis, and evaluate how things are going. Often, one parent may be completely unaware of something that concerns the other. The father may notice something about a child that has gone unnoticed by the mother, or may be able to give her a fresh outlook concerning a long-standing problem. Two people, sharing observations and brainstorming about possible solutions, are always more effective than a single person trying to do everything alone.

Of course, in some cases, you may not be able to sit down as a team to work things out. You may even be a single parent who has been forced to assume the entire responsibility for raising your children alone. The Bible states that the best scenario for a single mother is to be protected and assisted by men from the church. In today's world, that may be difficult to arrange. However, Jesus Himself has promised to pick up the slack. For those of you mothers who must try to get along without a husband for protection, support, and love, simply ask Jesus to fill the void and He will do it. He will be your ultimate authority, your covering, and your protector. Remember that you are never truly alone, no matter how much you may feel like it sometimes. (Also, if there are any single fathers reading this, remember that Jesus doesn't ever say His covering is only available for moms!)

The following chapters will examine the roles of the father and mother in more detail. Always remember that your own families have unique situations, personalities, and needs. Naturally, some of God's guidelines are unmistakable and unchangeable. However, within the framework He has given us, there is a great deal of room for individual variation. If something in the following discussion does not seem to fit with your own view of the family or the educational process, think through what will work for your own setting and for the players in your home school. Then act accordingly.

Chapter Eleven

The Father's Principle Role

"And He shall turn the heart of the fathers to the children and the heart of the children to their fathers, lest I come and smite the earth with a curse." (Malachi 4:6)

One of the reasons I hesitate to call the father the "principal" of the home school is that I believe his calling is far more important than that. God didn't call fathers to be the head of some institution that was designed by man. He called them to be the heads of their households. He told them to raise and educate their children and to instruct them in His Word (Deut 6:6-9). He told the fathers to discipline the children so that the mother's jobs would be more manageable (Prov 29:15). He told them to provide for the material needs of their families (I Tim 5:8). He told them to love their wives and bring up their children without anger and ill-tempered outbursts (Eph 5:33; Eph 6:4). In short, God has squarely placed the ultimate responsibility for every single facet of family life in the hands of the husband and father.

In today's world, this role as head of the household is often trivialized and disrespected. Almost every father on television and in books is portrayed as a lovable, bungling fool. This is true on every level, from the primary grade Berenstain Bear books up to the hit prime time television show, "Home Improvement." Strong, wise, competent fathers, like the ones on "Leave it to Beaver," "Andy Griffith," and "Father Knows Best," have become a part of our distant past, remembered only by trivia buffs and Nickelodeon fans.

I think some mothers share the blame for this reduced respect for fathers. Not only have some women attempted to usurp men's roles in the workplace, but they seem to thrive on tearing down their own households when talking with other women. Even among homeschooling mothers, I have often listened in disbelief as the women engaged in gossip, happily tearing apart their own husbands, discussing their shortcomings, and laughing at their "foolish" antics.

The Bible discusses relationships by setting up reciprocal roles and requirements. For example, the father is obviously intended to be the leader, the head of the wife. The wife, in turn, is supposed to be submissive to his leadership. However, this submission is based on the knowledge that the husband is expected to love her as much as he loves himself. Although the husband is clearly the leader, Jesus also says, over and over, that true leadership is obtained through serving others, rather than lording it over them.

When I asked my husband what I should say regarding the proper role of the father in the home school, he answered, "The husband's role is very simple...*whatever it takes.*" Whatever it takes to make sure that the household is functioning smoothly...Whatever it takes to fulfill his own God-given responsibilities...Whatever it takes to ensure that his wife is able to maintain her sanity and fulfill her own responsibilities...Whatever it takes in the way of time, effort, and involvement...That is the true role of the father in the home school environment.

Of course, the first and foremost role for the head of the household is to provide for his family. In our society, that often takes the father away from the home for many hours at a time. However, when the father and mother are clearly a unified team, acting together, the children will recognize that her authority is derived from his, and will continue to respect him even when he is not physically present. Above all, the mother must never join in any kind of rebellious spirit directed against the father during his absence. Since the mother and father are supposed to be "one," such rebellion is actually directed at herself and will tear down her own position within the household.

The father's role regarding the children is an all-encompassing one. He is expected to maintain discipline, teach character, act as a role model, and generally involve himself in their upbringing. Those fathers in the Bible who neglected this set of responsibilities, including some of the great Bible leaders like Eli, David, and Solomon, all suffered the consequences of allowing the mothers to do most of the child-rearing by themselves. However, fathers are expected to do more than discipline their children. They are expected to love them and understand them, so they can truly raise them in the *nurture* and admonition of the Lord (Eph 6:1-4). This requires that they turn their hearts back towards their children, their wives, and their households, and give these items a higher priority than fishing trips or football games.

Mothers have an enormous amount of responsibility on their shoulders, especially during the years when they are raising and educating several little children. They need their husbands around at night and during the weekends. It is totally unfair for men to go away for hours and hours every Saturday, leaving their wives alone an additional day of the week. This is true whether the absence is due to recreational outings or unnecessary overtime at work. Even if they simply "go away" by positioning themselves in an easy chair and immersing themselves in the game of the week, they are being immature and selfish. Such actions do not demonstrate a servant's heart, and will not result in a family where the wife respects her husband and values his leadership. Just as a wife tears down her own house when she tears down her husband, a father dismantles his own leadership role when he refuses to adequately shoulder his responsibilities when he is at home.

On the other hand, husbands are people, too, and have needs of their own. It is important for wives to recognize that husbands cannot be expected to work hard all day, and then come home and work all evening, attending to the needs of everybody else in the family. They have to have some time and space to do things that fulfill their own needs, too. That is why every role and relationship in the Bible is a reciprocal one. If the husband is supposed to be a servant to his wife, the wife is also supposed to be a servant to the husband. If the husband is supposed to do "whatever it takes" to make sure that the wife's needs are met, the wife is responsible to do the same for her husband. This might involve some compromising sometimes. It might mean adopting a spirit of giving instead of taking, especially when both players have needs that are hard to reconcile. Although an all-day fishing expedition or a weekly football marathon may be more than she can tolerate, the wife needs to realize that a few hours out on the riverbank or at a football stadium once in awhile might be exactly what is needed to rejuvenate her husband. That way, he will be a more effective, joyful leader when he is at home.

It is difficult for fathers to work all day, only to come home tired and ready for bed, and be deluged by people with concerns and problems. However, the fathers also need to remember that their children do not often get the chance to be with them during the daytime hours when everybody is productive and cheerful. The best scenario would be a change to a lifestyle that is more family-based. In our own family, we are working hard towards the day when Roy will be able to retire from his downtown office job and come home so we can all work together. Those fathers who must work away from home need to consider the picture they are painting for their children during the few hours they do spend together. If the fathers are constantly irritable and grouchy when they are at home, the children will not be given an accurate picture of what it takes to be a Godly man. If the children are rebuked whenever they come to their father with legitimate concerns, they will not be willing to listen to his advice when he finally decides to take the time to lecture them about something important. This is what the Bible is talking about when it says, "Fathers provoke not your children to anger, lest they be discouraged" (Col. 3:21).

One of the father's main responsibilities is to act as a role model in the home, especially for his sons. In all of his dealings, whether at home, church, work, or out on the baseball field, he needs to recognize that he is teaching his sons how to be men, and is showing his daughters what to look for in future husbands. If a father lectures his children about good sportsmanship and then turns around and acts like a two-year-old when he is watching a baseball game, his lessons will not be worth much. However, a Godly man can teach many things by example without ever preparing a lesson plan or lecture.

Fathers can also participate as a role model in academic areas. If little boys never see their fathers doing academic things, they will grow up believing that small children and mothers do "school work." They will never understand that true learning proceeds beyond the walls of the schoolroom, continuing throughout adult life. My husband taught our children to use an encyclopedia because he had the habit of using one himself. He taught them that real men go to libraries, because he often goes himself during his lunch hour. Unfortunately, he doesn't have the opportunity to go along with us on our weekly outings, but the children know that he values his library card and makes use of it on his own time. They see him reading at home, and they observe him writing letters to his friends. They watch him using math when he is doing his income taxes, and they observe whether or not he has a healthy spirit at the time. They see that he is interested in history and science, and they notice when he prefers a PBS special about the Civil War to a sports event or a situation comedy.

Except in special cases, most fathers don't have the time necessary to take on the responsibility of teaching specific subjects, especially if this implies some kind of a teacher-directed, lesson-plan-oriented nightly duty. Nevertheless, there may be some occasional academic duties that a father needs to do in order to assist with the smooth functioning of the family. For example, if the mother is totally illiterate in math, the father may need to occasionally play the role of math tutor after he comes home from work. If the mother is physically handicapped, has no car during the day, or is stuck at home with a sick child, the father may need to take the children to the library in the evening sometimes.

One of the most important roles the husband can play is the one he will probably find the most fulfilling. He can share his own interests with the children on a daily basis. My children have learned a lot of science during woodland walks with my husband, or by going along on a fishing trip and bringing the catch home to dissect. They never would have learned about crawdads in fish bellies from me. I have other interests that I share with the children, but they do not involve dismembering fish.

In some families, the wives may be the ones who cut up fish, and the husbands may teach the children how to sew. In some cases, the fathers will want to participate in curriculum fairs and support groups. In other families, the husbands will prefer to stay at home with the children so that the wives can have the time to take care of these responsibilities. In some families, the fathers may actually do a lot of the teaching, while the mothers may go out and earn some of the money that the family needs.

The specific roles may therefore vary tremendously from one family to another, but the "principle role" of the father always remains the same. He has ultimate responsibility for everything that goes on in the home. He must lead through example, through participation, and through service. He must be willing to do whatever it takes to make sure that everything runs smoothly. Although he is not the principal of a school, he is the ultimate earthly authority in the family, and that is a much more important role. As long as he has turned his heart back to his family, and recognizes the ultimate authority of God, his wife and his children will trust in his love for them and will feel confident about willingly placing themselves under his leadership.

"Every wise woman buildeth her house, but the foolish plucketh it down with her hands."
(Prov 14:1).

Chapter Twelve

Keepers at Home

The Bible contains far fewer specific instructions for mothers than it does for fathers. I believe that one of the reasons for this apparent lack of instructions is the Biblical emphasis on unity and the oneness of the married couple. In most cases, I think that the directions for fathers should also apply to mothers. Actually, almost everything that the Bible says about the father's role (other than his ultimate responsibility as head of the family) is also true of the mother, who is sort of an "appendage" of her husband.

This idea would probably give a lot of feminists heart failure, but actually being an "appendage" is a very liberating concept. Through total subservience, you can be shielded from some things that might interfere with your ability to be the emotional center of your family. Having a shield of protection enables you to do and be almost anything. When an irate neighbor comes to the door, or the authorities decide you are probably abusing your kids because you're so weird, isn't it a pleasant thought to be able to say, "You'll have to take it up with my husband?" I love to hide in his shadow sometimes. It's a very comforting place to be. Notice that such submission has not stopped me from getting an advanced degree, traveling around the country, writing and publishing books, and starting my own business. I've managed to "have it all" in a way many feminists only dream about, and it has come about precisely because of my subservient role. My husband's job has always supported us enough that I was able to play around, accomplishing many goals on the way. My husband has supported me and given me the freedom to do all these things primarily because his role has never been threatened or challenged. I have never had trouble accepting his leadership, either, because I am confident that he would never deliberately hurt me.

One of my first and most important roles, therefore, is to "do whatever it takes" to support my husband in his role. At times, this might mean cooking supper when I am dog-tired. At other times, it might mean going out and mowing the grass or changing a tire, or doing something else that is supposed to be the husband's job when he is too busy or tired to perform it. At times, it might mean standing up for him when others are criticizing him. Whatever it takes to support, respect, and accept the leadership of my husband...that's my most important job.

In addition to such wifely responsibilities, mothers are also expected to take a major part in the training, educating, and nurturing of their children. Some of the specific tasks of mothering have changed over the years. Since we spend less time on basic necessities in the modern age, we have more time to devote to helping with educational and vocational training for our children. However, the major responsibilities of motherhood have not changed significantly since the days of the Old Testament.

There are numerous examples of mothers in the Bible who are worth studying. There is Hannah, for example, who took her barrenness to God and asked Him for a son. Afterwards, she willingly gave Samuel back to the Lord, but she continued to demonstrate her love by sewing a new coat for him every year. There was the example of Naomi, whose love and caring extended not only to her two sons, but also to her daughters-in-law. There was Lot's wife, whose concern for her two married daughters that remained in the city of Sodom ultimately caused her to lose her own life.

Not every mother in the Bible showed good judgement at all times. Lot's wife should have thought about the unmarried daughters who were fleeing with her, obeyed God, and avoided turning into a pillar of salt. Even Sarah, who is often held up as an example of a virtuous wife and mother, made plenty of mistakes. She laughed when she was told she would have a son, and encouraged Abraham to doubt God by offering him Hagar in her place. Later she became jealous of Hagar and Ishmael, and caused her husband sorrow by demanding that he drive them away from home. There was Rebekah, who favored one child over another and tricked her husband, thereby separating herself permanently from the son she loved so much. We can learn a great deal from studying the weaknesses and mistakes of such women, as well as their strengths and successes.

There are two famous sections in the Bible that do speak directly about the role of the married woman. The first is Proverbs, Chapter 31, and the second is Titus, Chapter 2. Because I believe it is important for you to read both of these sections in their entirety, I'm going to quote them here, just in case you are reading this at gymnastics and don't have a Bible handy.

> *Who can find a virtuous woman? For her price is far above rubies. The heart of her husband doth safely trust in her, so that he shall have no need of spoil. She will do him good and not evil all the days of her life. She seeketh wool, and flax, and worketh with her hands. She is like the merchants' ships, she bringeth her food from afar. She riseth also while it is yet night and giveth meat to her household and a portion to her maidens. She considereth a field and buyeth it. With the fruit of her hands she planteth a vineyard. She girdeth her loins with strength, and strengtheneth her arms. She perceiveth that her merchandise is good, her*

candle goeth not out by night. She layeth her hands to the spindle, and her hands hold the distaff. She stretcheth out her hand to the poor, yea she reacheth forth her hands to the needy. She is not afraid of the snow for her household, for all her household are clothed with scarlet. She maketh herself coverings of tapestry. Her clothing is silk and purple. Her husband is known in the gates when he sitteth among the elders of the land. She maketh fine linen and selleth it, and delivereth girdles unto the merchant. Strength and honour are her clothing, and she shall rejoice in time to come. She openeth her mouth with wisdom, and in her tongue is the law of kindness. She looketh well to the ways of her household and eateth not the bread of idleness. Her children arise up and call her blessed; her husband also; and he praiseth her. Many daughters have done virtuously, but thou excellest them all. Favour is deceitful, and beauty is vain, but a woman that feareth the Lord, she shall be praised. Give her of the fruit of her hands, and let her own works praise her in the gates.
Proverbs 31:10-31

The other set of instructions for married women is found in the second chapter of Titus:

The aged women likewise, that they be in behavior as becometh holiness, not false accusers, not given to much wine, teachers of good things; That they may teach the young women to be sober, to love their husbands, to love their children, to be discreet,

chaste, keepers at home, good, obedient to their own husbands, that the word of God be not blasphemed.
Titus 2:3-5

These two passages of the Bible have probably caused more in-fighting among women of the church than all of the other passages in the Bible combined. Many women who work outside the home use the Proverbs example to brag about their lifestyles and mock "mere housewives," citing the stories of purchasing vineyards and delivering girdles to merchants. Yet all of these things can be done in a manner that is centered on the home. A woman at home might purchase an adjacent plot of land in order to plant a garden. She might sew during the evenings and take her garments to a consignment shop. She might bring her food from afar by shopping different stores for sale items, using coupons, and going to day-old bread stores or farmer's markets. None of these things implies that she is a professional realtor, seamstress, merchant, or buyer. In fact, I believe that this passage from Proverbs is clearly an indication that the woman is intended to center her life around the needs of her household. Many of her jobs appear to be supervisory in nature. She doesn't necessarily perform every needed task by herself, but she is the one who oversees their performance, assigns tasks, and checks up to make sure they are finished properly. Notice that this passage talks about the importance of the woman meeting her own needs, too. She is supposed to "gird her loins with strength and strengthen her arms," (get proper exercise and nutrition), and "make herself coverings of tapestry." Women are not asked to meet everybody else's needs without ever considering their own.

Note, too, that the woman in Proverbs is given acclaim and praise by her own husband and children. She is not encouraged to seek the acclaim of the rest of the world.

She is told to "let her own works praise her in the gate." She is clearly given instructions to keep busy, to concentrate on doing worthwhile things, and to let her husband, her children and her works speak for her if her worth is ever questioned out in the larger world. This passage is meant to free mothers from the pressures of trying to live up to outside standards. The only opinions that really matter are those of your own husband and children!

The woman in Titus, Chapter 2 is clearly labeled a "keeper at home." I personally believe that this is the role that is most appropriate for mothers to play. I believe most women would be fulfilled and happy if they chose this particular path. Being a "keeper at home" does not imply that your skirts need to be nailed to your doorstep. I consider myself a keeper at home, and I'm traveling to five different states this year to speak at curriculum fairs. That is very different, however, than having a full-time job where my hours and duties are dictated by somebody outside the family. I don't personally believe in mothers of young children working for other people outside the home in such a manner, unless they have *absolutely* no other choice in order to make sure their children are fed and housed properly. Still, despite my own beliefs, I have no plans to use this verse to condemn those who choose to take employment outside the home. When women attack each other in this manner, it always strikes me as judgmental and prideful.

Like the virtuous woman of Proverbs 31 and the keeper at home of Titus 2, the first priority of every woman should be overseeing the welfare of her family. However, since every family is different, there may be some mothers who can accomplish this goal while holding down an outside job. To insist there is only one Biblical method of accomplishing certain goals seems legalistic to me. The goals and priorities established by the father and mother, and the manner in which they submit these goals to the Lord are much more important than the specific ways they choose to meet them.

As much as I love homeschooling, I have numerous friends with outside jobs whose children are in institutional schools. I may not always agree with these women's choices, but they are fine Christian ladies nonetheless. To imply that they are less Godly than I am would be an exercise in prideful arrogance. Similarly, if I were to indicate that those homeschooling mothers who take a more structured approach to their educational efforts than I do have somehow missed God's best plan, I would also be overstepping my bounds. It's true that I believe God's best plan is a family, not a school. However, if your "family" winds up looking like a school after you have carefully considered all your options, that is perfectly okay with me! In fact, I just finished Alexandra Swann's book, *No Regrets*, which discusses her mother's incredibly structured style of education, which resulted in Alexandra receiving a master's degree at age sixteen. Although there were many areas where our methods differed sharply, I developed a great deal of respect for Mrs. Swann while reading the book. I found that we actually shared many beliefs and values, and have much more in common than our surface differences would indicate. After all, we both view homeschooling as a Christian commitment, we both center our lives on our homes, and we both want the best for our children. Aren't those the important things? What would it serve for people like us to argue over methods? Alexandra clearly states that she herself has "no regrets." If those methods worked for that family, for that teenager, and for that mother, more power to them!

There are some motherly roles that are shared by those who choose to homeschool and those who take other paths to their goals. For example, a mother is expected to protect her children when the father is absent. That might mean that she is with them constantly, or it might mean that she arranges for adequate, loving supervision when she cannot be physically present. She is also expected to provide a pleasant, beautiful, orderly environment for her family. This expectation is naturally tempered by the economic condition of the family and whether or not the children are around all day long tearing things up. Again, some women may fulfill this requirement by doing their own decorating and cleaning. Others may hire a cleaning service or delegate tasks to other family members. For homeschooling families, this expectation of cleanliness and order may need to be diminished at times in favor of more important priorities, like emotional health and sanity. The specific methods and the level of expectations may differ from time to time and from one family to another, but the basic assignments remain the same.

Finally, all mothers share the responsibility for being the emotional heart of the family and maintaining balance. In order to do that, every woman must make sure her own needs are addressed, so she is in shape to adequately meet the needs of the other members of the family. That involves getting sufficient sleep, nutritious food, and moderate daily exercise. It also includes finding time to continue doing things that are of interest to her, and making sufficient quiet time to study the Bible and pray. Many mothers are tempted to put their own needs on the shelf, thinking they are doing a favor for their husbands and children. Actually, such mothers are denying their husbands a well-rested, interesting partner, and denying their children learning experiences. (Remember the second form of motivation!) They will have a harder time building a genuine relationship with their children as they grow older. I don't want to have my children growing up thinking my only interests are cleaning, cooking, and chauffeuring them around. Why would they want to have any kind of long-term relationship with a marshmallow?

Special Roles for Homeschooling Mothers

As I have pointed out several times, I do not regard the home as a school. Therefore, I do not consider myself a teacher, except when I stand up in front of a group of ladies at a curriculum fair or workshop. At that point, I view my role as the "older woman" of Titus 2. (But not *that* much older!) When working, living, playing, and growing along with my children, my role is not "teaching" them. My roles include such things as setting appropriate goals, establishing an orderly home, maintaining emotional balance, sharing learning experiences with them, supervising their activities, observing their development, and stepping in occasionally to help fill in gaps or correct problems. In so doing, I wear a succession of hats, including those of "editor," "storyteller," "math tutor," and "chauffeur." If I thought of myself as a teacher, I'm sure I would start trying to plan and control everything as if I was in an institutional classroom. When I tried that in the past, it got in the way of true learning, so I learned to scrap such an approach in favor of a more natural approach to learning.

I believe that any homeschooling mother who adequately fulfills her responsibilities as a wife and mother will automatically also fulfill her responsibilities as a homeschooler. When neophyte homeschoolers ask me what kinds of roles I play in our day-to-day lives, I ask them to consider the roles that are taken on by a mother who is at home with her preschoolers and try to adapt those roles to the changing requirements of older children.

Mothers of preschoolers typically do not regard themselves as teachers. Nevertheless, they take their children on outings to the park, the playground, the zoo, and the library. They have the children in tow when they venture out into the community, doing their grocery shopping and going on trips to the post office and the bank. They play games with the children and read to them at night. They purchase materials that will encourage learning, such as blocks, educational toys, legos, and dolls. They occasionally pause to play along with the children, but they do not automatically stop their own lives in midstream in order to participate for four or five hours a day in their children's learning. They have some goals concerning the proper growth and development of their children, and constantly monitor their development to see if it appears to be on track. If children seem slow when it comes to walking or talking, the mothers may go to a professional for assistance or for a diagnosis, but they do not automatically turn over the decision-making process to that professional. They seek guidance from the Lord and make their plans accordingly. They set goals, observe progress, encourage growth, and fill in apparent gaps. They maintain balance by ensuring that the children do not become either over-stimulated or bored. In short, they supervise the raising and education of their children without ever becoming "teachers" or stepping out of their primary roles as wives and mothers.

The roles and methods that such mothers have used successfully for the first five years of their children's lives do not have to suddenly mutate just because those children magically turn six and become "school age." Remember that the concept of grade level was a creation of man. God never drew an arbitrary line and said, "Here is where everything is supposed to change."

The role I play as a mother of teens is remarkably similar to the one I had as a mother of preschoolers. The specific materials, methods, and experiences may be different, but the underlying purpose is the same. Nowadays, my teenagers may go to the library without me, but I am still trying to encourage them to read high-quality books and to enjoy the experience. Group trips to the park or zoo may have been replaced by individual experiences out in the community, but the basic reasons for such experiences remain the same. I am still trying to teach my children about the world around them and help them move out into that world in safe, manageable stages.

If you are a new homeschooling mother, there is no need to discover some special set of instructions that are needed in order to become a "teacher." However, there are many hats that you will wear during the course of working, living, and playing with your children on a daily basis, and some of these hats will be different for those of you who choose to keep your children with you all day.

First, in order to free yourselves from the idea of lesson plans, separate subjects, and grade levels, it is absolutely critical that you and your husband formulate some long-range goals to guide your efforts. Most of the specific roles of the homeschooling mother can be derived from looking at these goals on a regular basis. For example, one of my goals is to turn out eighteen-year-olds that love to read and write and are competent at these skills. In order to accomplish that goal, I must constantly monitor the progress of specific children (through observation, not necessarily through testing) and provide experiences and materials. My roles may include reading a bedtime story to a toddler; obtaining a magazine subscription for a preschooler; helping a six-year-old learn a few phonics rules; listening to an eight-year-old read "knock knock jokes" to me while I'm washing dishes; helping a ten-year-old write a letter to a penpal; editing a story for a middle schooler; or finding an appropriate resource to help a high schooler learn how to write a research paper. Some people might see such roles as "teacher" roles, but I don't. I just think of myself as a mother, who is helping her children set and reach worthwhile goals and doing "whatever it takes" to accomplish that.

One of your most important roles as a homeschooling mother is arranging your household in a manner that stimulates learning. The next chapter will address this matter in detail. Then, in part three of the book, we will get into more specifics about working with different age groups.

However, your own role will not really change much through time. It is basically the same regardless of the age of your children. You must love and understand your children, set appropriate goals for them, observe their progress, and search for ways to meet their changing needs. Sometimes this involves looking beyond the family for help, especially as the children grow older. The fact that you have elected to remain at home with your children does not mean that you must provide all their needs for them on your own for eighteen years. It just means that you must accept the basic responsibility for meeting those needs and act as a supervisor when other players are called in to help. Above all, you must never forget your main calling to be a wife to your husband and the emotional heart of your family.

If any of you feel too needy or burned out to serve in that capacity, you must stop what you are doing and back up until you figure out what it is you are lacking. Until your own needs are met, and you have discovered your personal joy and contentment, you cannot be an adequate mother or a responsive wife. If you are currently in need of assistance, always remember that you have a Friend Who has all the answers, and luckily, it isn't me!

Chapter Thirteen

Setting Up an Atmosphere for Learning

"Except the Lord build the house, they labour in vain that build it." (Ps. 127:1)

One of the mother's most significant jobs is to set up an atmosphere that is conducive to learning and growing. If such an atmosphere is in place, there is much less need to plan teacher-directed instruction, or to attempt to coerce learning. There are four elements involved in setting up this atmosphere: the setting, the people, the experiences, and the materials.

The Setting

The home is the base for learning and living together as a home-schooling family, but it should not be viewed as the complete educational environment. Homeschooling is not meant to be a confining way of life. It is meant to be a liberating lifestyle. Rather than being confined in a single room or building all day long, children are meant to work and play in the fresh air and interact with people out in the larger community. For that reason, the home school setting should not be viewed as a room in the basement that resembles a classroom in an institutional school. There isn't anything inherently wrong with having a room like that, but the setting is much broader than a single room. It is the community, teeming with interesting places and people and experiences: the parks, the churches, the grocery stores, the libraries, the nursing homes, and the zoos. Not only will a larger view of the home school setting enrich the lives of the children, but also it will help the mothers realize that they have not been removed from the mainstream of life. They have been freed, along with their children, to go almost anywhere they choose and learn anything that interests them.

Even though the community is going to be the larger setting for your homeschooling efforts, your actual home is going to be your base. As such, it is very important that it is set up properly in order to encourage meaningful learning. To begin with, it must be orderly, but not *too* orderly. John Dewey, who said a lot of things that aren't worth repeating, did manage to come up with one good line; "There is a certain amount of disorder in any busy workshop."

If you are the type of person who wants a "Better Homes and Gardens" type of household, you will either need to change or you will drive everybody around you crazy. That type of picture-perfect household does not work when it is lived in all day by a group of busy people. Many homeschoolers ask me how they can possibly get their housework done and still home school. I believe that most mothers who are experiencing problems in this area are probably making one of two mistakes: either trying too hard to act like classroom teachers while homeschooling, or trying too hard to maintain a standard of perfection in housework that can't exist side by side with a good learning environment.

A male lecturer once made the remark that he could tell whether or not a woman would make a good homeschooler by looking at the inside of her car. So can I, but I think we're talking about two different things. He meant he wanted to see cleanliness and order. However, if I see an immaculate car with six children inside it, I know that the woman has either a) *just* finished cleaning it or b) has a problem with being a perfectionist. Perfectionists have a difficult time homeschooling. Ultimately they will alter their behavior and their expectations, quit homeschooling, or drive their families crazy.

Naturally, the Bible does indicate that order is a good thing. A completely disorderly, sloppy home is not a good environment for learning, either. Both extremes will lead to problems. I believe in the adage, "A place for everything and everything out of its place at least some of the time." Underlying order is critical. If things don't have a "home" when it comes time to straighten up, nobody knows what to do with anything. However, if a home is always neat as a pin, it suggests that too high a priority has been placed on things, rather than on people.

As the mother of a nineteen-year-old, I've learned a little bit over the years. One of the things I've learned is that I spent too much time on housework when Sam was little, and turned his failures in that area into too big an issue. Keep your priorities straight. There are few enough moments to enjoy with your children. Don't spend every morning doing battle with them over the need for picture-perfect bedrooms. Although it is true that developing good habits is an excellent thing for which to strive, the quest for neatness should never be allowed to deteriorate into a war between the perfectionists and the wayward geniuses in your household.

There are many books out there that talk about how to get rid of clutter. They make a lot of good points. For those of you who are serious pack rats, it might be a good idea to adopt some of their suggestions for having less junk around, but a really clutter-free home is also going to be a learning-free home. All that clutter serves a good purpose sometimes. You can't build a decent cave without having some old sheets around. You can't let a six-year-old girl "make a patchwork quilt", (which involves a lot of cutting and destroying and no actual patchwork quilt) without having a box of material that nobody else cares about. You can't have a home business that will help the children learn important skills without having boxes and papers piled up in your bedroom from time to time.

Of course, there is a difference between clutter and filth. A degree of clutter is necessary sometimes if you are going to be working and living together at home. However, I don't believe in allowing filth to accumulate. That's why I always set priorities for housework, and try to accomplish at least a little every day. That way the bathrooms won't sit for days with that stuff growing in the toilets, and the kitchen cabinets will not be taken over by bugs.

Every morning, I try to think through a few goals for the day, and assign some priorities. I consider what types of learning experiences we will probably be doing that day, what sort of professional or personal things I need to be doing, what external appointments we have, and what is most critical in the housework department. That way, the one or two most pressing jobs always get done. The laundry doesn't pile up for weeks, the dirtiest rooms get cleaned, and the biggest messes get picked up.

In some homes, the desire for perfection comes from the husband. In those cases, it is the husband that will have to become more flexible if he is going to help his wife retain her sanity. He will either have to be willing to pay for outside help, clean himself when he comes home from work, or understand that his wife's biggest responsibility relates to the children, not the material things that make up the household. As always, consideration on the part of both players is the key. My husband and I have faced this issue over the years. He has gradually begun to understand that complete order is beyond my capability. However, I have made it a point to ask him what items drive him craziest when they are not done. After much thought, he decided that he gets the most upset when he reaches into his drawer and doesn't find clean clothes, or when he comes home at night, fully prepared to help me out by cooking supper, and finds a messy kitchen. Therefore, I have assigned kitchen cleanup and laundry the highest housework priorities.

There are also seasons for priorities. Sometimes, when I'm writing a book or the children are off on a tangent that involves the use of several rooms for caves and railroad depots and grocery stories and libraries, the housework may really take a beating for awhile. Then I'll look around and say, "Okay, enough is enough. Time to get this place looking decent again." The priority becomes housework for a couple of days at that point, and there may be little or no "education" taking place. Yet, isn't housework part of life and learning, too? Both boys and girls will need to know how to use a vacuum cleaner, work in the kitchen, repair clothing, and mow the grass. To me, these are important learning experiences, and I have no problem including them on an evaluation report.

One problem with a degree of disorder is that it tends to make everybody kind of tense and irritable. That is one reason I always have one area of the house that I try to keep looking like one of those "Better Homes and Gardens" rooms. Then, when someone needs a dose of peace and order, they have a place to go. I also believe in the need for beauty. For example, I am sitting in my bedroom right now, working on the computer. It's messy in here. There are stacks of newsletters waiting to be mailed, piles of laundry sorted and waiting to be washed later in the day, and a new shipment of laser paper that broke open on the truck. However, I recently used some money I earned in my business to put down new carpeting. Seeing the lush, blue carpet under the laundry makes me happy. The plants on the windowsill and the bird feeder outside contribute a little bit of extra color. The Monet print on the wall gives me something to look at besides the clutter. There is a display of seashells that reminds me of a happy time on the beach. With such beauty surrounding me, I can overlook the temporary mess. I also know that when I do have the time to clean, I will have an absolutely gorgeous room, one that really could be photographed for a magazine. (But don't send the cameras over anytime soon.)

Setting Up Learning Centers

One method of encouraging learning in your home is to set up "learning centers" similar to those used in kindergarten classrooms: an art center, a science center; a music center; a center for dramatic play, etc. I've written a guidebook on this subject that is available through the "Relaxed Home Schooler Newsletter" or from the Elijah Company. In it, I explain the idea of setting up small areas of your house on a theme basis. This type of center can be extremely effective at stimulating learning. For example, we have an art center in our kitchen. On the wall is a bulletin board for the artwork. Under the counter, behind closed doors, is all the clutter that accompanies an art center: paper, brushes, paints, etc. On the counter itself is a display of art books, usually borrowed from the library. Sometimes it really looks pretty and well organized. That's on a good day.

Now let's talk about real life. Sometimes, the top of the counter has groceries on it. Sometimes the kids take all the thumb tacks to stick stuff up on their doors and the bulletin board is bare and I have no idea what happened to the lovely art creations that were there. Sometimes the paint spills and I don't notice it for a couple of days until the dog discovers it and tracks it into the living room. I have always had this dream of running an article on learning centers in one of the major homeschooling magazines and including two pictures: one the way it should be set up, and one the way it often looks in reality.

The fact that the center doesn't always look like it's set up for "Show and Tell Night" doesn't diminish the fact that it is a wonderful way to encourage art, however. When people come over to my house, after having read my guidebook, they are usually surprised to see how few actual discernable centers I have set up. Trust me, we do not look like a kindergarten classroom. As far as I'm concerned, learning centers are more of a state of mind sometimes than a physical reality. When I encourage people to consider setting up learning centers, I'm trying to get them to grasp the concept that learning materials need to be put down low where children have access to them and permission to use them. When a variety of interesting items are readily available, learning will eventually happen. In fact, many of the learning experiences at the art counter have occurred after the counter has become extremely messy. When it's time to clean up, the kids will often re-discover a book or some materials that they had forgotten about. The center will look picture perfect for ten minutes and then a new project will start up.

When considering your learning environment, also remember to include the outside areas of your home. Even on a small city lot, there may be room to plant a garden, create a sandbox or sandpile, attract birds and butterflies, or build a picnic table. In the mornings, after I've made my list of what to accomplish that day, the next thing I do is to look outside and see what the weather is like. It if is really pretty, I know I might as well tear up the list. The best part of homeschooling is flexibility. There is no way you will find me scrubbing my bathroom floor or asking a young child to sit inside all morning doing academic work when it is seventy degrees, the sun is shining, and the garden or the park or the zoo is beckoning us to come and join the fun.

The People

When I was a young mother, before I ever even thought of myself as a homeschooler, I used to get pretty lonely sometimes. Before my marriage, I used to be quite busy and popular, and never had a scarcity of people with whom to talk. At first, the home environment, with only a young baby and toddler as discussion partners seemed rather stifling. Gradually, however, I realized that the only real reason for my loneliness and boredom was my unwillingness to step out of the house and move out into the larger community. (Somebody once said, "If you're bored, it's because you're boring.") The world was waiting for me just outside my door. All I had to do was stop focusing on how much trouble it was going to be to get the kids ready and load up my car and go somewhere to meet some interesting people.

One of the major criticisms of homeschooling revolves around the lack of "socialization." Personally, I believe that school children are at a serious disadvantage when it comes to socialization. They are stuck in one room for much of the day, dealing only with people who are exactly their own age. In many cases, their interactions are severely restricted, even within this group of peers. The emphasis is on quiet and order, rather than on meaningful interaction. (This isn't true of all classrooms or all teachers, naturally. There are always exceptions.)

Homeschoolers can have the whole world as their classroom, if they learn to take advantage of their freedom to move about during the day. Many of our best learning experiences have revolved around the people we meet out in the community. Our children have been involved in community theatre, sports leagues, gymnastics lessons, private school enrichment classes, church activities, volunteer placements, apprenticeships, and many other organizations over the years. They have met interesting people of all ages and walks of life, and these people have enriched their lives beyond measure. Just the other day, my older son went to a small shop in downtown Atlanta where there was an eccentric old man who had roomfuls of wood. He loved that wood so much he taught my son all about the various types and grains available. There's no teacher more effective than an eccentric old man with a burning interest!

For those of you with small families, this need to get out into the community is even more pressing. When your own family circle is rather small, there is less opportunity for shared enthusiasm, and the learning experiences are bound to be narrower in their scope. For example, our family is naturally attuned to the fine arts and literature. When my oldest son became interested in higher-level science, we had to search for other people to use as resources. He may never have even discovered his love for science if we had not exposed him to people and places beyond our front door when he was still a young child. He needed to have a wide variety of experiences in order to discover his own interests and talents.

The Experiences

In order for young children to gradually discover their own talents, they need to be exposed to a wide variety of people, places, and experiences. However, these experiences should widen their world in a gradual manner. At first, preschoolers need to have their parents around in order to feel secure enough to benefit from activities. They do not need to take all kinds of individual lessons in order to make the most of their creativity at this age. Formal training in gymnastics, baseball, art, and music can all wait until the upper elementary years, unless the motivation for such lessons really is coming from the children and you are able to go along on a regular basis.

However, as a family unit, it is important to get out and experience a wide variety of things when the children are young. Taking them on small field trips that consist of one or two families is usually much more effective than going on large-scale outings. On these larger outings, the children are usually so engrossed in the other children that they learn little from the experience itself.

Some experiences that don't appear educational on the surface are also valid learning experiences. Going along on trips to the bank or grocery store, visiting dad's office, fishing at the state park, and hunting for leaves in a neighbor's backyard are all valuable times for sharing.

In the upper grades, children will gradually find those areas that interest them. At that point, they need to be given the opportunity to develop their talents through lessons and more formal, individual experiences. Later on, in the teenage years, such experiences might include apprenticeships, volunteer work, and paid work experiences. I have even known some teens that started their own businesses. Adopting the belief that the classroom is the wide world outside our four walls has resulted in a tremendous amount of learning. However, timing is critical. Pushing too many experiences on young children can backfire, especially if the children are not really ready to move out on their own and parents push them into situations they cannot handle. It is also important to maintain balance, both for individuals and for families. Too many individual activities can wind up reducing family togetherness and burning everybody out.

The Materials

When I said we hardly ever purchase curriculum materials at the beginning of the year, you may have thought that we have very few materials in our home. Nothing is further from the truth. We just purchase these materials a little at a time over the course of the year, as learning opportunities present themselves. Recently, when Laura expressed an interest in learning something about Egypt, we got out the Greenleaf Press catalogue and ordered some materials on that subject. A recent interest in insects led

Steve to go to the library to take out books on grasshoppers and cicadas. Many times, when we go on field trips, we wind up buying all kinds of books and materials at the museum store. We also spend a lot of money on magazine subscriptions and books. Every time we go to the mall, a favorite stop is the bookstore, where we buy a few new items to add to our family library.

The key to providing a rich environment is to keep everything low and accessible to the children. It also helps to rotate items so things don't start fading into the woodwork. A new toy or book will often arouse fresh interest in learning. New materials at the art center will stimulate new projects. A new aquarium, or a few new fish in an old aquarium, will probably start a flurry of learning about aquatic life. A new book, thrown casually on the sofa, will often be read without the need for coercion or external motivation of any kind.

When money is scarce, many materials can be obtained through free sources, including the public library. Most libraries have a variety of materials that they loan to patrons in addition to books, such as tapes, videos, toys, or pieces of artwork. Some companies also have free materials that they will send on request. I have one friend who spent an entire month sending off for information from every company she could think of. She received so much literature in the mail that she had to buy a used filing cabinet to keep it all organized! Government offices and chambers of commerce are also good sources for educational materials. We have obtained information on trees from the forestry service, gardening from the extension office, and animals from the educational office at the zoo.

There are certain "school-like" resources that you may also want to obtain as funds permit. These include items like globes, wall maps, microscopes, telescopes, encyclopedias, computers, dictionaries, and a variety of other resource books, such as field guides, atlases, and Bible concordances and commentaries. Some of these make good gifts to request from grandparents. The rest can be obtained slowly at new or used book fairs. It might also be a good family project to do a series of fundraisers to get money for a desired piece of equipment. Schools and churches are not the only ones who can sell candy, wash cars, or run a rummage sale. Such a fundraiser could be a valuable learning experience in itself.

When materials are still scarce, it is time to remember, once again, that the home is only your home base, and is not your entire "classroom." The world is your classroom. There are maps and encyclopedias at the public library. There are telescopes available at astronomy clubs and observatories. There are Bible commentaries and atlases available in the church library. A lack of funds does not have to result in a less effective educational setting. However, if you are confined to your house for any reason, whether it is a lack of a second car, or a remote setting, or a physical problem, you need to figure out some way to get around such difficulties. (In Matthew 17:20, the Bible promises that all such mountains can be moved!) Somehow or other, you've got to be able to make use of the wider world around you if you really want your children's education to be rich and varied.

Part Three:

Down to Specifics

"Shew me thy ways, O Lord, teach me thy paths."(Ps. 25:4)

"Though the Lord be high, yet hath He respect unto the lowly..." (Ps 138:6)

Chapter Fourteen

Respecting Children as Individuals

Up to this point in the book, I believe that everything I've said has been solidly based on Biblical principles and generally applicable to everyone. Once we start discussing specifics, we enter the realm of educational philosophy, and some of you may not agree with everything I say. That doesn't bother me in the least. After you put this book down, you may feel like I went off the deep end in this section. That just means you will be one step closer to figuring out what *you* believe about education, and that is the most important thing.

However, no matter what we each believe about education or what style of teaching fits in best with our particular interests or personalities, we must always remember that education is an individual affair. Our children are all unique. I may be "the relaxed home schooler," but I have at least one son who is "type A" all the way. Some children need more structure than others do. Some are flexible, floaty geniuses who need lots of space. Others are organizers and neat-niks, and will try to provide their own rigid structure if nobody else provides it for them. Children also have different timetables for learning, and do not all learn in the same manner. For all of these reasons, what works well with one child may practically destroy another one in the same family. The beauty of the homeschooling situation is that we can adapt our techniques and methods for each of our children, provided we don't get so hung up on our own beliefs and styles of teaching or discipline that we forget to treat them as individuals.

As parents, no one knows your children as well as you do. That is what qualifies you as an expert when it comes to working with them. There may be a few things about education that you don't know, but you do understand the most important thing: what makes your individual children "tick." You already know their strengths and weaknesses, personalities, and interests. Now you need to learn a little bit about developmental stages and learning styles, so you can get a better handle on what is normal and what might constitute a problem at each stage of development.

As far as I'm concerned, many of the lines that have been drawn by man are artificial boundaries which can easily be ignored. Such artificial lines include the ones between "preschool" and "school," and between "adolescence" and "adulthood." However, there is one major shift that occurs at about the age of twelve that cannot be ignored. People who don't understand this shift generally have a great deal of trouble dealing with their teenagers. For that reason, I have devoted most of the chapter on young teenagers to a discussion of their special developmental needs.

I believe that most people could avoid the troubles associated with the junior and senior high school years by seeing their teens as young, transitional adults, rather than as some kind of a special class of adolescents. Teenagers in our society continue to need our protection and guidance until they leave the home. However, they also need to be treated with respect and gradually moved out into the larger community so they can begin the process of developing their own judgement, learning to look for the Lord's guidance for themselves, and finding a direction for their future lives.

In the Bible, we are shown very little about Jesus' early childhood. The first glimpse we have of him after the manger scene occurs when he is twelve. I don't think this was a coincidence. Earlier than twelve, children are in need of parental sheltering. Like baby birds, they aren't ready to fly yet. When children reach their teens, the role of the parents begins to take a different turn. The responsibility to shelter and protect young children gives way to a need to gradually and gently push them out of the nest. When mother eagles believe their babies are ready to learn how to fly, they deliberately shake up the nest in order to make it less comfortable. There comes a time when true love for our children makes it necessary to do the same.

In our society, however, people tend to push children out of that nest too fast. Many parents give children an unbalanced childhood by requiring too much of them and giving them too little free time to enjoy. Then, just when they are in need of new experiences in the adult world, the parents try to hold in the reins too tightly. Rather than allowing their teenagers to slowly move out into their adult roles, they treat them like children long beyond the time when such treatment is proper. The result of this schizophrenic attitude towards children is easy to see in American society. Many of the six-year-olds are busy trying to act like teenagers, and the teenagers themselves can't seem to grow up.

In the following pages, we will discuss each of the stages that children pass through in their development. Each is a unique stage, with special needs. Understanding a little about development will help you to figure out the best methods and materials to use for each age group. However, please remember that each person is a special case. Each individual was created by God for a particular purpose, and is worthy of our respect, regardless of his or her age. If something I say doesn't jive with your own knowledge of your children or teenagers, don't listen to me! After all, I have never met your children, so I can't treat them like individuals. Use your own judgement. Learn as much as you can, but adapt that knowledge as necessary to fit your own situation. Never change anything after reading a book or listening to a tape unless you first search for your own guidance and become convinced that something is right for your particular family. Remember: You are the experts, because you know your children better than anyone else. God entrusted them to you because He trusts you, and He will help you make proper decisions at each stage.

Chapter Fifteen

The Preschool Years: 0-4

"Suffer little children to come to me, and forbid them not, for of such is the kingdom of God."
(Luke 18:16).

The term "preschooler" is based on one of those assumptions about education that we were discussing in an earlier chapter. It implies that there is a magic line that children cross at the approximate age of five or six. Before children reach that age, most people assume parents automatically know how to raise and educate their kids without much assistance. After that age, education is usually turned over to the realm of professionals.

One of the stated goals of "Education 2000" is that all children will enter school "ready to learn" by the year 2000. On the surface, that sounds admirable, but what does it really mean? Children are born ready to learn. How exactly will these educational "experts" assess whether or not six year olds are adequately prepared for school? They will do it by stepping across the artificial boundary and pushing their "expertise" on parents of preschoolers. Eventually, if enough parents allow this to happen, the boundary itself will no longer exist. At that point, the burden of proof will shift. In order to be allowed to raise their children without accepting professional assistance, parents will have to demonstrate their capability. That will eventually lead to some kind of special education in parenting, complete with a required diploma.

Unfortunately, many parents have already accepted the belief that they are not capable of dealing with their preschoolers adequately in a natural fashion. The concept of "readiness training" has permeated our society. Programs like "Sesame Street" were originally aimed at disadvantaged children. Such kids often need special outside experiences in order to compete successfully with children like yours, who have been involved in natural learning experiences at home. Over the years, however, such programs have convinced parents that all children need to have these formal learning experiences. Parents of preschoolers have seen hundreds of workbooks sitting on the shelves at the discount stores. They have been conditioned to believe that they must teach a long list of "readiness skills" to their preschoolers in order to adequately prepare them for crossing a nonexistent boundary at the magic age of six. Most parents in our society believe attendance at preschool is also crucial in order for children to compete successfully with their peers.

Do any of you really believe that you must develop specific strategies in order to teach children to cut with a scissors, color and paste, recognize the front from the back of a book, or learn their numbers and their ABCs? In a normal household, with children of average intelligence, you'd have to shackle the kids and keep them in a closet to prevent them from learning such things by the age of six. "Readiness skills," although necessary for some disadvantaged youngsters, are absolute hogwash in most families like yours. Children are ready to learn when they are born. All you need to do is to provide a stimulating environment, along with a little loving guidance, and the learning will never stop.

Within the homeschooling community, there is an additional controversy over whether it is better "late than early", or "never too early" for certain types of learning experiences. I'm often asked which side I endorse. The answer is "neither and both." It always depends on the methods used and the individual personalities and needs of the specific children involved. I agree with much of Raymond Moore's research, as detailed in his books, *Better Late Than Early,* and *School Can Wait.* Many small children, especially boys, are not ready for certain structured educational group experiences until they are well past the preschool years. That was one of the main reasons we became homeschoolers in the first place. However, despite the fact that our oldest son, Sam, wasn't ready for a group setting at the age of six, he had begun reading on his own at the age of three or four. I would have had to punish him and hide the books to stop him from learning to read. Not all children are ready at that age, however. Our youngest son, Steve, is six years old now and is just starting to read on his own. I've known other perfectly normal children who still weren't reading at the age of ten.

Decisions concerning methods and proper timing must all be based on common sense and your knowledge about your own children. Some of them are going to be ready for certain experiences earlier than others and some will need extra time and patience. Trust your intuition. Try something. If it works, that's fine. If you sense that your children are unhappy and are bucking you, don't automatically assume it is an issue of disobedience or laziness. Just put the work away for awhile and try again some other time in a slightly different fashion. You don't need a bunch of child development experts arguing over methods or telling you when or how your children can learn best. You know those kids better than anybody else. You can figure out what works and what doesn't work for each of them as individuals, and you can sense when the timing is right and when it isn't.

As usual, the specific methods you decide to use in your home will determine much of the interaction that takes place. One of the questions I am frequently asked by parents of young children is, "How can I homeschool with preschoolers around all day?" If homeschooling means sitting down for four hours with your older kids and looking like a school, it may be difficult to accomplish with preschoolers around. If it means learning and growing together as a family, then it shouldn't be that big a problem. The youngest members of the family may be more interested in learning than the older ones, so it won't be very hard to bring them into the family circle if you are reading interesting stories and doing active projects together. However, it may be trickier to keep them out of that circle on occasion, when you feel the need for a little privacy or an activity that requires too much sitting still.

Toddlers can be extremely demanding. Even without attempting to look like a school, parents can get exhausted from simply trying to keep children safe at this age. Older siblings can get frustrated, too, if they are unable to finish projects or have any kind of personal space that doesn't get violated by toddlers. For that reason, it may be necessary for you to re-design your home and re-consider some of your priorities in order to live and work together without excessive conflicts. If it is at all possible, everyone in the household, including the mother, needs to have at least one small area to call his or her own. When I had small children, my house looked like a maze of barricades, but there were very few of the structures that most people use to exert control over children: cribs, playpens, swings, and walkers. Of course, we were given most of these items in the beginning, but we rarely used them and they eventually wound up being sold at a garage sale.

I don't believe in confining toddlers in playpens. I'm the type who would rather sit in the playpen myself, surrounded by my books or my computer, and let the toddlers play in the rest of the room. I used to dream of designing a huge crib for myself to work in, and allowing my child to roam around the rest of the area unfettered. If I could get a patent on this idea, I'd be a rich woman. Every one of us needs to know that there is at least one area that is off-limits to everybody else. As mothers, we need our quiet spots. You know how you value your bathtub. That's because it is the only place where you hope you will be allowed to sit for a few minutes undisturbed.

Your older children have the same need to have a special place of their own. If they have their own bedrooms, either allow them to have their rooms locked on occasion, or put baby fences in all the doorways. If your children must share a room with a younger sibling, consider barricading one small section so they have at least a little privacy. All children need a place where they can build a structure without having it knocked down. All of them need a quiet spot to read a good book, even if the spot has to be outside under a tree. If you provide your older children with a little personal space, and can learn to trust them to be productive without constant supervision, you can take turns getting away from the little ones once in awhile. I used to ask one of my two older children to supervise the younger kids for an hour a day while I did a few sit-down activities with the other one.

The adults who live with toddlers and preschoolers also have a need for an occasional break from these little people. This is a very intense age, and most mothers need to get away for awhile occasionally in order to recharge their own batteries. This is especially true for mothers of boys. Don't feel guilty if you feel the need to hire an occasional babysitter or take a preschooler to a "mother's day out program" once in awhile in order to spend time with your older kids or have a couple of hours for yourself. If you are not comfortable with either of these options, consider hiring an older homeschooler as a "mother's helper" a couple of mornings a week so you can have a little assistance without actually being away from the children.

Other than the need for such an occasional break, however, life is so much more fun when the little ones are included in all the adventure and excitement of learning. Most three or four year olds are big enough to be involved, especially when workbooks and textbooks are put aside in favor of relaxed unit studies or real life experiences. The babies and smaller toddlers may be too little to understand certain things, but they will want to be included anyway. You might be surprised if you realized how much they are picking up along the way.

Babies and toddlers don't need a lot of "educational experiences", but they are certainly learning a lot from what is going on around them. They are building their personalities and their attitudes towards life during these early years. Children this age need security and protection. They need to be with their mothers. They need *quantity* time. They need to learn that their needs are going to be met in a consistent manner. What they don't need is some supposed "expert" convincing their mothers that the babies must learn how to live on a schedule or go for hours without the comfort of their mother's arms in order to develop order or build character.

I believe that babies need to have their legitimate needs met when they first feel them, not when some adult caregiver dictates. When my first son was born, I didn't know much about taking care of infants. I believed the doctor when he said my baby was nursing too frequently. I gave Sam the apple juice in order to free myself up from one feeding and wound up giving him constant diarrhea and colic. I left him in a crib to cry instead of picking him up when he needed me, and wound up making him insecure and unhappy. I am so sorry that I gave him such a rocky start. He cried so much and I felt like crying most of the time, too. It is hard for mothers to listen to their children cry. There's a reason for that. God made babies cry so that we would go to them and comfort them and fulfill their needs. Babies were never meant to lie alone in a crib so they could learn to go to sleep on their own and somehow build character in the process. Sam came into this world requiring very little sleep. He was alert and curious almost all day and all night long. God made him that way, and He did it on purpose. I was the one who messed up because I believed the books that said all newborns were in need of a certain number of hours of undisturbed sleep. I should have just realized that Sam was different and asked God to teach me how to be an effective mother, but I didn't know any better at the time.

As I gained wisdom and experience, my other babies gradually nursed longer, slept with me more, and were held constantly instead of being placed in plastic contraptions. I have learned that if children have their needs met when they are young, they will grow up to be enthusiastic, capable, independent youngsters. Don't listen to those supposed "experts" who sing a different tune. Listen to your mother's heart, and you will automatically know what to do.

There are two main controversies when people start talking about very young children. The first relates to issues of security, such as feeding schedules versus demand feeding and cribs versus family beds. The second concerns the need for intense learning experiences versus a more natural approach to development. Everybody wants their children to be smart, and everybody knows that a good start is critical for proper brain development, but there are big differences among the methods and materials used to accomplish that goal.

I don't believe in heavily structured, teacher-directed activities at any age, but I think such activities are the most damaging when forced on tiny children. Babies don't need to have flash cards flipped in their faces in order to stimulate proper brain development. There have been experiments conducted which proved that rats in a natural environment learned more and had better brain development than those who were being trained by experts in an artificial environment. I doubt that God made human babies less capable than rats.

All of the hints about preparing a learning environment that were given in a previous chapter are true for life with preschoolers, too. Given the proper experiences, materials, and people, they will naturally grow and learn. If there are safety scissors available they will learn to use them. If there are crayons and paper around, they will create pictures and other objects of art. Through such activities, their fine motor skills will develop in a natural manner, without any need for teacher-directed lessons. If children are given the opportunity to run and play in the out-of-doors, they will also develop their gross motor skills in a natural manner. If you take them to the library on a regular basis and read to them every night before bedtime, they will learn all they need to know about books without requiring special training in "reading readiness" skills. If they are provided with appropriate games and other learning materials, they will gradually learn their numbers and letters without needing structured workbook exercises. If they have people around who are willing to listen to them and talk to them (without talking down to them), they will learn the basic communication skills. In short, if there are plenty of experiences, materials, people, and social interactions available in their environment, the learning will occur in a natural manner, without the need for a great deal of advance planning.

When creating an atmosphere for learning, there do need to be safety precautions built in when there are babies and toddlers around. There is never a substitute for constant supervision, but it can help if you structure your environment in a safe manner. If you have a two-year-old, sharp or poisonous objects need to be stored out of reach of tiny hands. This may limit their accessibility to your older children, but it needs to be done. Small objects that might constitute choking hazards need to be kept inside some of the barricaded areas. Legos and other toys with small pieces need to be kept in an older child's space where the younger ones can't go. I realize most of you already understand this need for safety, but I have seen people forget such precautions when they get excited about setting up learning centers for their older children.

Of course, when you are there to supervise activities adequately, preschoolers need to learn how to use some of these materials, too. They also need to experience a wide variety of people and places. This doesn't necessitate a lot of group experiences or private lessons at this age, however. Family outings are definitely preferable to either individual lessons or participation in large group outings. Unless the children themselves are strongly motivated in a specific area, I don't believe in rushing certain types of experiences. My youngest child, (who is six years old), is taking gymnastics right now, but he watched my older daughter and pestered me for months before I relented. Most of the preschoolers in such classes are there because their parents think it will be a good experience for them. In my opinion, romping at the park as a family is a much more worthwhile activity for the vast majority of young kids than taking structured lessons or participating in group experiences.

Although it may be fun for a child to have a friend over once in awhile, I don't believe it is really necessary to get the kids together with a group of same-aged children on a regular basis. A lot of people think I'm crazy when I talk this way. They see me as some kind of mutant child development expert. Since I have a Ph.D. in early education and child development, I am supposed to *know* how *important* these experiences are for socialization purposes. Bah Humbug. I can provide better socialization experiences by taking the kids with me wherever I go. I don't feel the need to expose them to constant illnesses by taking them to every group activity under the sun, even those at my own church. We go to a large institutional church, where almost everybody else attends the public school. I don't want to spend the entire week weeding out the influences they would get by attending all of these social functions, so my younger kids sit in the pew with us and attend very few "preschool" activities.

The thing that amazes me is that the very same people who come up and compliment us on the wonderful personalities and behavior of our older kids are simultaneously trying to change our minds about how we treat the younger children. I keep wondering, "Why do they think our older kids turned out so great? Do they think it was a fluke?" These people are seeing the difference between teenagers who were raised the way God intended, in a family setting, and those who were raised in herds. Even seeing the difference, however, they still believe in the need for those herds.

Chapter Sixteen

The Primary Years: 5-7

Most homeschoolers realize intuitively that they are already doing a great job with their preschoolers. However, many parents have internalized the nonsense about the arbitrary line between the preschool and primary years. As soon as children reach the age of five or six, many parents still think that they must choose between turning them over to outside educators or beginning to act like teachers themselves. Being a mother or a father somehow isn't perceived as being "good enough" anymore once the first grade rolls around.

As far as I'm concerned, the mother's role doesn't need to change significantly just because her children reach school age. Specific methods and materials will gradually alter as the children become ready for new experiences, but the basic role of the mother remains the same: protecting her children and providing them with guidance; setting appropriate long and short-term goals; observing their progress; staying alert to notice possible gaps or difficulties; making sure appropriate materials, people, and experiences are available; maintaining balance; and managing the routine affairs of the household. There is no need to suddenly add in such roles as "lesson plan maker," "test grader," or "lecturer," which are more appropriate for classroom teachers than mothers.

The specific suggestions found in this chapter should not be limited to the primary years. They should be a continuation of previous experiences, gradually building on the knowledge and skills that the children are developing.

Life is a continuum, and there is no need for sudden mutations in methods, goals, or materials as the children pass from one stage to another.

Natural Literacy

The main traditional goal for the primary years is to develop competency in reading and writing. Keeping in mind that some children may not be ready to learn to read or write until later on, let's discuss some of the ways to encourage the development of natural literacy during these years.

In my opinion, learning to read and write is a natural process, which does not require heavily structured, teacher-directed activities and lesson plans or expensive curriculum materials. In a literate home, in a literate society, learning to read and write should be as natural as learning to walk or to talk. I never consciously set out to teach any of my children how to read or write. We simply read books together, starting when they were just babies, because we enjoyed the experience. I answered their questions and had a few cheap phonics materials around in case they needed them. For the most part, they learned on their own, each in his own way and on his own timetable. However, it didn't just happen by magic. There are certain things that must be in place in order to foster such natural development.

First of all, you must make sure your home is a truly literate environment. In order to do this, you need to recognize that one of your primary jobs is to act as a role model for your children. If they see their parents using communication skills as a normal part of adult life, most children will want to read and write themselves, and their own motivation will cause them to work toward that end. You need to spend some time reading yourselves, and do some writing on a consistent basis. The specific books or writing experiences you choose are a personal matter. You don't need to be reading classical materials, or submitting articles to magazines. You may prefer to read homeschooling magazines and write letters to your relatives and friends. The important thing is that the children see you using these skills in a way that is meaningful to you.

Similarly, the children need to see that you value the time that you spend at the library. When you go there, be sure to pick out a few items for yourselves. Let the children see you learning to use the card catalogue or asking the librarians for information. Fathers need to be involved in this process, too. If little boys never see their fathers going to the library or reading for their own enjoyment, they will grow up thinking library trips are for women and little children, and will never develop the habit themselves. Again, the fathers don't need to feel like they have to take out specific materials. Old fishing magazines are just as good as books by Charles Dickens for this purpose.

In a literate home, there should also be several magazine subscriptions coming to the house. Every member of the family, from preschool age on, should have at least one magazine coming in his or her own name. Over the years, we have taken a lot of the money other people spend on curriculum and purchased books and magazine subscriptions with it. Among the magazines we have enjoyed are the following:

Science: "Ranger Rick," "Your Big Backyard," "3-2-1 Contact," "National Geographic," "Zoobooks," "Nature Friend."

English/Writing: The "Cricket" series: "Babybug," "Ladybug", "Spider," and "Cricket"

History: "Cobblestone"

Homeschooling: "Homeschooling Today," "The Teaching Home," "Home School Digest," "Home Education Magazine," "Growing Without Schooling"

Kid's homeschooling magazines: "Thumbprints," "Kids at Home".

Adult magazines: "National Geographic," "Country," "Birds and Blooms," "Reader's Digest," "Guideposts."

Some of these magazines are Christian, but others are secular. When questionable magazines come into the house, we generally try to glance through them before we give them to the children. We do very little actual censoring, but I always want to know what my kids are reading, so we can discuss anything that might be objectionable. I do censor occult influences, especially when the children are younger, including stories about witches and Halloween. I often have to throw away October issues for this reason, or do a lot of cutting and pasting before handing them to the children. However, within the boundaries we have set for acceptable materials, I believe in allowing the children to read what they are interested in, rather than assigning them specific books or magazine articles and turning reading into a structured learning experience. Keeping their motivation alive is much more important to me than teaching a list of unrelated "skills" or focusing on reading comprehension.

The whole idea of teaching "reading comprehension" strikes me as a bunch of nonsense. If the children are reading something on their own initiative, they probably understand most of the material. If they don't understand something completely the first time they read it, they will probably understand it better at some later time. Why would they continue to read things they couldn't comprehend? Unlike the classroom teacher, who is dealing with thirty students at a time, I don't have to ask my children to prove to me that they understand something. They don't have to demonstrate that they have read materials by filling out mindless book report forms or answering comprehension questions. I can see them lying on the couch, and I know whether or not the material is keeping their attention. At one point, I thought I might use Charlotte Mason's technique of "narration", asking the children to narrate the story to me after they had read it. The first couple of times, they thought that was kind of neat. Pretty soon though, they spotted it for what it really was: one more educational technique. The more I live with my kids, the more I realize that focusing on anything except the enjoyment of reading just diminishes their desire to read the next book or magazine article. When that desire stays alive, the necessary skills will develop in a gradual manner.

Another part of establishing a literate home is to incorporate family "story hours" and individual reading sessions into your normal daily routine. I have always been careful not to try to "teach" reading during some kind of "school time," so the children don't start to view reading as an unnatural activity that requires special training. The children do a lot of their own reading during the day, usually following a period of strenuous outside play, when they feel like curling up and doing something quietly. Our family story hour usually takes place just before bedtime. I do some of my own reading or writing in the morning before breakfast. The children have been instructed not to disturb me at that time unless there is an emergency. As a result, I have noticed that they often use this time for doing some of their own academic work, such as writing or studying, especially as they grow older.

In addition to establishing a literate home, there are three other things that must be considered if you want your children to develop their reading and writing skills in a natural manner. These are: readiness issues & individual timetables for learning; learning styles; and issues concerning motivation. We have already discussed the fact that not all children are ready to start actual reading at the same age. Keep in mind, however, that learning to read is a continuous process that begins long before the children can actually pick out words in a book. They are already learning to read when they are sitting down next to you on the couch listening to a good book. If you continue to read to them, take them to the library, provide them with appropriate materials and experiences, and answer their questions, the reading skills will develop gradually without a lot of specific intervention on your part.

We have always had a variety of materials available for our children when they were learning to read, including some cheap phonics workbooks and homemade phonics games. However, it is a mistake to emphasize the study of phonics with all children, because not all children learn well in this manner. It is very important for you to consider your children's learning styles when attempting to help them learn to read and write. A good way to begin is to picture your child sitting next to you on the couch. If the child tends to stare off into space and appears like he is not paying attention, he may be an "auditory" learner, who is taking the information in through his ears. This is the type of student who will later sit in a college class with his arms folded, listening to the teacher, and not take any notes at all. Auditory learners often drive their classmates crazy, because it looks as if they are not even listening, but they often get the highest grades in the class. Auditory learners are usually also the students who will do particularly well with phonics, because they can "hear" the sounds better than other learners.

The child who always wants to sit next to you, needs to see the words and the pictures on the page, and wants to read the same books over and over (especially when they are approaching the stage of beginning to read themselves) is often a "visual" learner. In later life, visual learners are the ones who take a lot of notes and need to have some kind of material on the blackboard in order to follow the teacher's lecture. When somebody is reading something out loud to a visual learner, the person often grabs it away, saying, "Let me see that." Somehow, it is almost impossible for some highly visual learners to take in information through their ears. For that reason, phonics is often very frustrating for them. My daughter, Ginny, was like that. If I had insisted on phonics, she never would have learned to read, (or possibly might have been labeled "learning disabled"). Instead, we read *Downy Duck Grows Up* one million times and she gradually memorized every word in the English language. Her lack of phonics did not prevent her from getting a 97th percentile on the verbal part of the PSAT at the age of fourteen, or from becoming a voracious reader and a highly-skilled writer by the time she was a young teenager.

The third type of learning style is the "kinesthetic," or "hands-on" learner. This is the child who wants to play with legos or drive trucks around the living room while he is listening to you read. Of course, sometimes such behavior is just an indication that the child is not ready to sit still and listen to a story yet. However, some people are highly kinesthetic and remain that way into adult life. The adults who are "hands-on" people tend to go into careers where they work with their hands, such as carpentry, plumbing, or sewing. Kinesthetic learners can sometimes be helped by adding in hands-on experiences, such as making sandpaper letters, arranging blocks with letters on them, or using a variety of games, such as "Scrabble" and "Upwords" to help them learn their letters and recognize words. However, like all children, the best "technique" is no technique at all. Simply read them interesting, high-quality books; respond to their questions; try out a few phonics lessons when they seem like they are ready; back off if they obviously aren't responding; and stop trying so hard to act like a teacher. Providing a literate environment and acting like a mother is completely sufficient. Keep in mind, too, that some "hands-on" children can actually pay *more* attention when you allow them to keep on playing with their legos during story time than if you insist on having them sit next to you with their hands folded in their lap.

The final thing that must be considered when encouraging natural literacy is the issue of motivation. In the schools, children's motivation is often dulled. Every two-year-old has a high level of motivation for learning, but sometime before the age of ten, most children in our society have had their internal motivation smashed.

I believe in reading for the sake of reading, and using writing as a natural form of communication. Whenever reading is broken down into separate skills and children are required to dissect stories, answer a million questions, or do book reports, their motivation is dimmed. I remember how much I hated *Moby Dick* when I had to read it in high school. I could have read the entire book over the weekend, and probably would have enjoyed it. However, I was forced to read it over a period of two months, one chapter at a time, answering questions and considering the symbolism until it made me sick. I never use books in this manner with my children. If there is something I want them to understand, we may discuss the book together. Once in a great while, I might ask them to tell me about the story, or even write something about the book, but this is rare. In general, I allow my children to read whatever they like (within the boundaries that are acceptable to our family), and leave them alone to enjoy their books without turning them into educational experiences. Using this approach has resulted in a high level of reading competency in our family. My ten-year-old is currently reading, *Sense and Sensibility*, and *Pride and Prejudice*, by Jane Austen. These books are, quite frankly, considerably more sophisticated than my own selections. Ginny, my sixteen-year-old, has read virtually every major classical author in existence. (Of course, both girls have also consumed their share of "Babysitter's Club" books). The boys tend to read more non-fiction than fiction works, but they also go on occasional classical binges. Last year, Dan was reading short stories by authors such as O. Henry and Nathaniel Hawthorne. Sam has been reading Shakespearean plays lately, and both boys enjoy the works of C.S. Lewis and Frank Peretti. None of these books have ever been "assigned" reading.

In the schools, after the children have had their own motivation ruined, teachers often step in with external motivators to try to get it going again: stickers, happy faces, grades, trips to amusement parks, pizza parties, summer library reading programs, etc. I avoid these so-called "motivators" like the plague. All they do is give the kids the subconscious message that reading is something they need to be bribed to do. Eventually, children who are motivated by such "carrots and sticks" will have these external motivators removed. By that time they will have forgotten they ever had another reason to want to read or write. That's why so many students in our society view the end of "school" as the end of learning. My most important goal is not to turn out competent readers or writers, although each of our children has attained a high level of competency anyway. My main goal is to turn out adults who *love* to read and to write. Without such an attitude, skills themselves are pretty useless.

Primary Math

During the primary years, it is important to lay down a solid understanding of basic number concepts in order to ensure that children will be prepared for a more serious study of math in the upper grades. Like the skills of reading and writing, this understanding can be developed in a natural manner, without the need for structured workbooks or assignments.

By the age of eight, most children should understand and be able to perform simple computations, such as addition and subtraction. Many will be ready to learn "regrouping" (carrying and borrowing) and beginning multiplication by the later primary years. The development of simple measurement skills, the ability to tell time on both digital and traditional clock faces, and a basic familiarity with fractions are also desirable. All of these skills can be developed through normal daily experiences.

The first thing that needs to be accomplished is to develop a solid understanding of numbers themselves, both the numerical symbols and the quantities that they represent. Many young children can impress the adults around them by reciting the numbers all the way up to 100. This does not indicate a real knowledge of what these numbers stand for. In order to develop a genuine "number sense," children need to have lots of concrete experiences with counting and working with a variety of real-life objects. Simple experiences, such as setting the table for five people, dividing candy into equal portions for their younger siblings, or helping with the baking and the grocery shopping will teach these concepts without the need for lesson plans or curriculum materials. Try to use a few math terms, like "one dozen," or "a half a cup" when the children are helping you in the kitchen or the store, so they can gradually learn these terms in context.

If you are going to use curriculum materials during the primary years, the best ones are often those that are based on manipulatives. However, if these courses are too expensive, you can easily create your own manipulatives using cheerios, raisins, or Popsicle sticks. I particularly like to use Popsicle sticks when the kids are learning how to carry and borrow, because they can be bundled into groups of ten and then taken apart and turned back into "ones." We used to take a big sheet of paper and make three columns for the ones, tens, and hundreds, and use these Popsicle sticks to do problems. First we did the problems with the sticks, and then we wrote out the same problem on another sheet of paper, and I showed them how to do the actual computation.

There is no real need for workbooks at this age. However, if children enjoy workbooks, there is nothing particularly wrong with using them, either. Just remember that many of the workbooks contain problems that are not really appropriate for this age group. Unfortunately, the publishers of most math books have taken what is known about children's cognitive development and pushed it down a few notches, to try to force early learning. (You know what happens when you try that with potty training!) In many cases, children are not ready for many of the experiences in these "primary" workbooks, especially when done in an abstract manner on a piece of paper. Primary-aged children often have the most difficulty with number lines, workbook exercises that involve time, money, or measurement, and problems that are "turned around" (3 + ___ = 5; rather than 3 + 2 =___). We always just skipped those types of problems and either substituted real life experiences or put them off until later on.

Five-year-olds are not too young to learn about measurement, time, and money, provided that these things are taught in a concrete manner, during the course of everyday life. If you want your children to learn how to tell time, buy them a watch and ask them what time it is every once in awhile. When they don't answer, bend over and say, "Oh, it's six o-clock. That's almost time for supper." Try not to overdo this type of thing, and try to speak normally, not in an artificial "teacher" voice. Kids catch onto your motives real fast!

Measurement can best be taught through real life activities like gardening, baking, woodworking, and sewing. There's no need to add in the metric system at this age unless you're planning a trip to Europe. That can come later. Other number systems can wait, too. It's hard enough to learn about one system at a time. (My children did gradually learn their Roman numerals at this age, because we often read books that had chapter titles that used these numerals.)

Money recognition and counting can be fostered through either giving the children an allowance or having them earn money by doing chores. Be sure to also teach them about tithing and saving as soon as they have any money of their own. My six-year-old doesn't have any need to learn about pennies, nickels, and dimes from a workbook, because he counts his money almost every day. I hope that means he might be an accountant someday, rather than a budding "Scrooge."

The development of math skills can also be fostered by using a variety of games, such as Cathy Duffy's "Beginner's Math Mouse Games," and "Math Mouse Games," or "Muggins," and "Knock-Out," by Old Fashioned Products. My children have also enjoyed using "Learning Wrap Ups" to help them develop speed with math facts, although we don't emphasize the development of speed until the upper elementary years. Personally, we have found "wrap ups" to be preferable to flash cards, since flash cards have the potential for turning into a battle of wills between parents and children. (Wrap ups are self-correcting, so the parent does not have to be an active participant.)

If you do decide to use some workbooks at this age, we have found that those purchased at discount stores are often just as useful as those put out by curriculum suppliers. The most important thing is to make sure that the children themselves enjoy these workbooks. They usually like those that are colorful, have understandable pictures to go with the problems, and limit the number of types of problems that are found on one page. Again, watch for problems that are too difficult for the children at this stage, and don't make them finish every single problem on the page if they seem particularly frustrated. If you have already purchased a large math workbook from one of the curriculum suppliers, you might want to consider Xeroxing or cutting out a few pages at a time to give to the children, so they don't become overwhelmed at the task that appears to lie ahead of them.

Primary Science

During the primary years, science instruction should mainly focus on helping the children develop a love for the out-of-doors and an appreciation of God's world. We have spent a lot of time going on nature walks, building a nature trail in the woods outside our door (complete with a "trail guidebook"), and making a variety of collections. Most children this age are also interested in the stars, the sun, and the moon, so we have focused a little on learning about astronomy. In addition, we talk about scientific issues when we hear or read about something in the paper. This past few months, we have been discussing comets and meteors, since the comet "Hale-Bopp" has been clearly observable from our porch every night.

The children have learned about birds by making bluebird feeders, maintaining various suet and seed feeders on our property, and keeping the bird bath filled. We have a number of field guides inside the house, so we can look up birds or insects we don't recognize. We also talk about the differences between different types of creatures. (Examples: Mammals have fur, give birth to live babies, and nurse their babies. Birds lay eggs, have wings, and have been given different beaks depending on the specific ways they use them. Insects have three body parts and six legs, and may either be harmful or beneficial to the garden, depending on what they eat. Spiders are not insects, but are actually related to scorpions, and eat meat rather than vegetables, so they are helpful in the garden.)

We don't do any structured experiments at this age, but we try very hard to find answers to the questions that children come up with on their own. "Why does the soap float?" "Why does the moon change shape?" "Why does a ball roll down hill?" "How does the traffic light know when it's time for us to go?" In order to answer such questions, we have a variety of resource books on hand. If we can't find the answers in our own books, we go to the library to look them up. However, this is not nearly as useful, since children want answers to their questions immediately. If they have to wait a week to find out the answer, they may have forgotten the reason they asked the question in the first place.

Another activity we have enjoyed is visiting hands-on science museums. We seldom go with organized groups, because we have found that these museum trips are pretty worthless unless we are able to stay for an entire afternoon and mess around with things on our own. We have often selected one museum or zoo per year and purchased a family membership, so we could go over and over again until we knew all the exhibits by heart.

Books, magazines, and nature videos have also added an important dimension to our science education. We prefer to use library books on single scientific topics, rather than textbooks, which rarely go into enough detail to keep anyone's interest alive. When our oldest son was sixteen, he took the GED and earned a 99th percentile in the area of science, despite never having taken a structured course in biology, chemistry, or physics. When asked how he did it, he stated, "I learned everything I know from watching nature videos and reading my magazines." Of course, he was particularly interested in the area of science. Access to those same materials did absolutely nothing for Ginny. Her lack of interest in science was one of those "gaps" that I needed to eventually address, but I waited to worry about it until long beyond the primary years.

Primary Social Studies

During the primary years, the social studies curriculum in the public school typically focuses on developing a knowledge of the surrounding community. If you have adopted the extended community as your "classroom", you probably won't need to worry about meeting this need. However, you may want to plan a field trip to an elementary school some time, since this is probably the only place your kids won't go on their own.

We focus primarily on learning about American history during these years, through reading good books rather than textbooks. At this age, we focus on interesting historical fiction books, biographies, and poems. Examples: *Ben and Me*; *Paul Revere's Ride*; *George, the Drummer Boy*; *The Battle of Bunker Hill*; *The Drinking Gourd* and biographies of presidents, explorers, Indian chiefs, soldiers, and statesmen. One of the few textbooks we use in the lower grades is the Abeka third grade social studies text, which I usually read to the children during the primary years. This is an excellent collection of read-aloud biographies of famous Americans.

We have also watched a variety of television shows or videos about history, including the miniseries "Centennial," "Roots," and "George Washington." These videos and books often stimulate relaxed unit studies, which we'll discuss in the next chapter. In addition to using good books and videos, we try to go on a number of historical field trips every year. We have been to Civil War battlefields, forts, history museums, and living history encampments, among other things.

Geography has been taught through real life experiences, (including traveling to curriculum fairs!) and through playing with puzzle maps or geography coloring books. When Sam was in college, he became embroiled in a heated debate over whether or not Louisiana actually touched the Gulf of Mexico at the mouth of the Mississippi. He knew he was right because he had put our puzzle together so many times that he knew how the pieces fit together. (Incidentally, make sure your puzzle maps are correct, or they might teach the wrong things, and *that* will be difficult to get out of their minds.)

Other Subjects

Other subjects that we learn about during the primary years include Bible, art, music, and physical education. We teach Bible truths in many ways. We have always had a Bible story hour in the morning at the breakfast table. Usually, when the children were younger, we used story books rather than the Bible itself. Occasionally, this presented difficulties when the stories were "dumbed down" too much, had historical inaccuracies (a Brittany Spaniel on the Ark, which wasn't developed until centuries later), or had too much teacher-directed material thrown in. One of the best exercises I've ever done with my own kids was to fold a bunch of papers together and make a little "book" for them to draw pictures of the Bible stories as we read them, along with short captions. By the end of the year, they each had their own little "Bibles" they had written and illustrated themselves.

Our art and music have been fostered through the use of learning centers. In our art center, we have a variety of raw materials and art supplies, a bulletin board to display the latest creations, and a shelf where we display a book about an "artist of the month." (I get a new artist book each time we go to the library.) Our music center has a variety of tapes and CDs, including those by classical artists and a variety of other musical styles. We also have a number of real musical instruments, including a piano and (unfortunately) a full set of drums. The children are taught from an early age that they can use these instruments only if they treat them with proper respect. Most of our children have learned to play several instruments, simply by having them available to play. We have waited until the children were older to allow them to take formal lessons.

As far as physical education goes, most children have their needs met through engaging in outdoor exercise and occasional trips to the park. We have a basketball goal outside and keep the usual array of bicycles, skateboards, and baseball equipment in an outdoor storage building. The occasional "couch potato" may need a little extra motivation to get out and get some exercise, but most children are naturally motivated to play outside if given the time and a few basic materials.

By the time children reach the end of their primary years, the following are some of the experiences they would have had in the public schools and the typical skills they ""should have mastered," (according to the authorities). I thought you might like to see something like this as a sort of reference, but please don't use it to plan instruction. Keep in mind that some children may learn these skills later than others, so don't worry if they are not all in place by the end of the primary years.

Language arts: Basic skills in reading; ability to write short one-paragraph reports, letters, and lists; decent, readable handwriting. (Personally, I emphasize the communication, not the handwriting, and allow my children to use the computer for writing as soon as they express the desire to learn to type).

Math: Number recognition; basic adding and subtracting; carrying and borrowing; simple understanding of fractions; knowledge of time, measurement, and money.

Science: Basic terminology and concepts, especially those dealing with nature; participation in a variety of hands-on experiences.

Social Studies: Recognition of the 50 states, the continents and the oceans; some knowledge of major events in American history, such as the Revolutionary War and the Civil War; knowledge of the community and community workers, and a development of the appreciation of diversity, by which they mean homosexuality is normal, etc.

Bible: Ha. Public schools don't care what you know.

Art: Basic skills with coloring, gluing, cutting, etc. Few public schools focus on art appreciation at this age.

Music: Basic music notation; knowledge of instruments in the orchestra; knowledge of a few classical composers; development of singing ability and sense of rhythm and pitch.

Physical Education: Development of fine and gross motor skills (fine motor skills are things like the ability to use a pencil and scissors; gross motor skills are abilities like running, skipping, hopping, etc.); exposure to a number of group sports, like kickball, soccer, softball, and basketball; development of the ability to push, scream, holler, and shove when involved in intensely competitive organized activities.

Extracurricular: Development of the ability to "just say no," coupled with the provision of many opportunities to use this skill on a daily basis.

Chapter Seventeen

The Upper Elementary Years: 8-11

"Even a child is known by his doings, whether his work be pure, and whether it be right." (Prov. 20:11)

The period from about eight to eleven or twelve years of age is usually a delightful one. Most children of this age are happy, industrious, and interested in everything that is going on around them. Their willingness to study is increasing due to their lengthened attention span. The bouncy six-year-olds are gradually turning into calmer, more sedate ten-year-olds. Even late readers are usually beginning to catch up by the end of this period, and are ready for more scholarly learning experiences. For these reasons, many parents who formerly focused on reading together as a family and learning through real-life experiences wind up switching over to a structured, textbook-workbook approach at this point. For some people, this might be an acceptable choice, but we have followed a different route.

Like many other home educators, I've been influenced greatly by the work of Charlotte Mason. Like Mason, I despise textbooks. Textbooks are usually quite boring. Some are too easy and others are written in obscure, difficult language. They usually cover topics in such a superficial manner that nothing of real value is learned. Rather than giving the children contact with the great minds of our civilization, such textbooks expose them to the minds of the average people who edit them. These editors often select what they think are the important things for the children to learn; change the words of the great authors to make them more "understandable" (i.e. dumb them down) and intersperse their own ideas, which may be of questionable merit. We rarely use textbooks in our family, except as resource materials. Occasionally, if one of the children expresses a desire to purchase a particular text, we will still do so. However, my personal feelings echo Mason's thoughts on the subject:

> I know you may bring a horse to the water, but you cannot make him drink. What I complain of is that we do not bring our horse to the water. We give him miserable little textbooks, mere compendiums of facts, which he is to learn off and say and produce at an examination; or we give him various knowledge in the form of warm diluents prepared by his teacher with perhaps some grains of living thoughts to the gallon. And all the time we have books, books teeming with ideas fresh from the minds of thinkers about every subject to which we can wish to introduce children. *School Education,* 1907, p. 171.

Instead of textbooks, Mason believed in using what she called "living books," whose worth had been tested through time. She read young children the unabridged classics. As they grew older, they developed their own excellent taste in literature and began to read the great books themselves Her expectations for children were quite high, and she was seldom disappointed. Believing that children were capable of reading the classics without much difficulty, she noted:

> A special literature for children is probably far less necessary than the

booksellers would have us suppose. Out of any list of the 'hundred best books', I believe that seventy-five would be well within the range of children of eight or nine. *School Education, 1907, p. 122*

In addition to the classical works of literature, Mason believed in exposing the children to the best of modern materials. In today's society, she would undoubtedly be amazed by the vast amount of children's literature that has sprung up. Many of these books are insipid, dull, dumbed-down, and worthless. At least a third of them advocate questionable values that would have astounded Mason. However, there are also many worthwhile books available at the public library and through local booksellers. Such books would provide a much broader, in-depth type of education than one that is based primarily on the use of textbooks. After all, there is a reason that textbooks are considered secondary sources of information. That is why I believe one of the most worthwhile things new homeschoolers can do is to learn as much as possible about literature (both adult literature and children's literature), so they can make informed choices about read-aloud books and can learn to supervise their children's reading experiences.

As my own children grew older, I continued to read to them, selecting books that were a little too difficult for them to read on their own. Together we devoured such books as *Huckleberry Finn, Watership Down, Swiss Family Robinson, Johnny Tremain, Robinson Crusoe, and Heidi.* I also encouraged them to read whatever they enjoyed during their free time, and made absolutely no assignments in this area. Sometimes they got stuck in a rut, such as a "Babysitter's Club" rut or an "Encyclopedia Brown" rut, and eventually I had to step in and ask them to read some alternative selections. However, we continued to view reading as an important part of everyday life, rather than as a "school subject." As a result, all of our children have developed the skills associated with reading and writing. They have learned to appreciate great literature and have developed a high degree of discernment when it comes to separating the wheat from the chaff. Most important, they have retained their love of reading and learning as they have grown older

Focusing on Goals

In *The Relaxed Home School,* I discussed the need for setting goals for children in the areas of values, attitudes, habits, skills, talents & interests, and knowledge. In our family, we tend to emphasize the first three categories during the preschool and primary years. By the time children enter the upper elementary years, they have generally developed good attitudes toward learning and a variety of worthwhile academic habits. Such habits include reading for enjoyment, looking up information when they don't know it, and going to the library on a regular basis. Their values have also developed during the early years, and a solid foundation has been laid in the areas of character and religious training. With the children well on their way to achieving these goals, our attention now typically begins to shift towards the development of skills, talents & interests, and knowledge.

This is the age when we begin to focus on the development of specific skills, such as learning to use the library for beginning research purposes, learning to use reference materials such as encyclopedias, maps, and dictionaries, and starting to develop computer skills. However, we have not found it necessary to adopt a heavily-structured, teacher-directed style of instruction in order to accomplish these tasks.

Our children have primarily learned to use encyclopedias because they saw their grandparents using them. They have learned to read maps because we frequently take out maps to determine the best route to take on family trips, or to look up places we hear about on the nightly news. They have learned such skills as alphabetizing and using guide words a little at a time, when they actually have a reason to look something up. Of course, these skills don't just develop all by themselves without a little bit of thought and role modeling on the part of the parents. Whenever our children ask us questions, my husband or I pull out an encyclopedia or other reference book to help them locate the answer. As we look up some information Laura wants to learn about breeds of dogs, we muse, "Let's see, that would be in the "D" encyclopedia." Then we take the D volume out, and page through the book, saying, "D—Da—De—Do—now we should be getting close…here it is – D-O-G-S." As usual, we try very hard to do this kind of thing in a conversational, incidental manner, rather than putting on some kind of a "teacher voice" and making it seem like a contrived learning experience.

Relaxed Unit Studies

In addition to reading together and allowing the children to follow their own individual interests, we often use what I call "relaxed unit studies" at this age, especially in the areas of social studies and science. Our relaxed unit studies often are stimulated by one person's current interest. Sometimes they are triggered by a good book or video. The next step is usually going to the library to look up additional books or videos on the subject. Often, as the children get older, these interests become the subject of a writing experience. While I may suggest such activities to my children, I rarely force them to write if they are resistant to the idea. Once again, developing the attitude of loving to write is a more important goal to me than the development of specific skills. As long as the children are reading widely by this age, and are listening to me read good books to them at least a few times a week, I am confident that they will gradually learn to write without much difficulty.

The relaxed unit studies we utilize usually follow a fairly predictable pattern. A book, video, or individual interest triggers a learning experience. The other siblings often get involved, although I try to respect the individuality of the children and don't insist on 100% participation if the others are busy with alternate projects. We go to the library, get out a bunch of books on the subject, and read them together. Sometimes the research we do gets transferred into a piece of writing; sometimes it doesn't. Many times, the children will be motivated to participate in some "hands-on" activities that are associated with the study. Occasionally, we may go on a couple of related field trips. Then, about the time that other unit study people are really cranking up for the major "culminating experience," our studies die a more natural death. Typically, they either fade away into the woodwork or trigger a related unit study. One interest melts away and another takes its place.

Occasionally, this approach has been criticized by people who are concerned that children will not learn to stick to tasks or finish things if they are allowed to let projects peter out before they are "done." Personally, I've always believed that perseverance and responsibility can be learned better through work and community experiences than through contrived educational activities. For example, when my son comes in halfway through mowing the lawn, he knows he can take a break or get a drink, but he also knows he is expected to go back out and finish the job. When my daughter is responsible for doing the laundry, she knows she can't just stop in the middle and leave the clothes in the dryer to get wrinkled. When my oldest son has an outside job, he learns very quickly that he is expected to show up for work on time every day and stay until his tasks are completed.

To me, it is more effective to teach such "work-related" skills in the context of real work. As far as academics go, I try to keep learning fun and enjoyable. I'd rather switch to a new area of study and keep attitudes enthusiastic than continue with a project after the interest has died.

One pre-planned unit study that we have used several times is Valerie Bendt's, "Creating Books with Children." This unit study has helped our children learn about the processes of writing, editing, typesetting, illustrating, and bookbinding. Those children that have the ability and motivation to stick with the project until completion wind up with a nice momento, a hard-cover book with a book jacket that actually has their own picture and biography on the inside flap. When children lack the motivation to finish a large project like this, we sometimes do smaller projects, instead. At times, I have simply stapled several pieces of typing paper together, or bought a blank manuscript book at a curriculum fair. A new booklet with a lot of blank pages has often stimulated writing with the younger children. We don't necessarily have to do massive academic projects every year in order to encourage creativity in this area.

By this age, some children are also motivated to write articles to submit to real magazines or newspapers. There are several children's magazines, such as "Kids at Home," and "Thumbprints," which are home-school based and accept children's writing. Real newspapers may sometimes publish children's work if the kids are writing about something important or interesting, and if the work has been edited and polished. My oldest daughter once submitted an article about a real dog that was being used in a community production of "Annie," and had a friend take a photo to go with the article. It was published in the paper the next day. The editor made no changes at all, and I doubt highly that he even realized that a child had submitted it.

Many parents believe that if they do not specifically teach their children the proper rules of grammar, punctuation, and spelling, there is no hope that they will ever learn to be competent writers. However, it has been my experience that children who read well will usually develop excellent writing skills by the middle school years. (Sometimes, boys can be quite slow in this area, but they often make tremendous strides when they finally get serious about their writing.) Although I occasionally work with my children as an editor, using common sense and emphasizing their good points rather than their mistakes, I do very little in the way of serious instruction until they reach the teen years. Again, I am much more concerned with avoiding "burn-out" through the use of endless workbook exercises, than I am with "covering" all the bases in the area of language instruction. Charlotte Mason seemed to partially agree with my assessment in this area. Concerning the need for "teaching spelling," she once wrote:

> It is impossible to teach children to spell when they do not read for themselves...but in thousands of cases that come before us we find that children who use their books for themselves spell well because they visualize the words they read. *Towards the Development of a Christian Philosophy of Education*, 1925, p. 271.

Of course, the ability to spell is partly dependent on learning style. Those who are visual learners will often start out as terrible spellers, but will gradually correct all their errors on their own, simply because, as Mason said, they "visualize" the words they read. Those who are auditory learners may continue to attempt to spell words phonetically. Some of them may eventually need to learn some rules in order to improve their spelling, since English is not really a phonetic language. However, in my opinion, this type of instruction can wait until the children reach their young teens and their own motivation provides the spur to improve specific writing skills. Often, many problems will correct themselves in a natural manner if parents emphasize reading for enjoyment during the younger years, and wait a little while before emphasizing such writing skills as grammar, spelling, punctuation, and capitalization. Most people jump on the "instructional bandwagon" far too early, and wind up destroying the children's attitudes. This approach can result in very competent sentence-diagrammers that have no interest in using their writing skills in their real lives outside of school.

Studying Social Studies Using Relaxed Units

Most of the social studies that we do during the upper elementary years revolve around relaxed unit studies. At some point, I do believe in studying both American and World History in a more linear fashion, starting at the beginning and going up to modern times, but we usually postpone that until the teenage years. For those who adopt the "unit study approach," it may help to have a time line on the wall, so you can gradually learn where each subject fits into the grand scheme of things. Of course, we don't have one, but it does *sound* like a good idea, doesn't it?

A classic example of a relaxed social studies unit study is the one we did on medieval times. It was originally triggered by watching the musical, "Camelot."

(Note that we did not purposely watch the video as a motivational device. We just like to watch musicals!) Following this video, Ginny became absolutely fascinated with this time period in history. She asked if she could go to a camp that featured a medieval theme. That camp experience led to a continued interest that lasted about three years. At some point, she read the book *Ivanhoe*, and we studied about the Knights of the Round Table. That study stimulated the boy's interest, and they began to stage mock sword fights and to dress in knight costumes. As the study ebbed and flowed over the course of several years, my children all gradually learned everything they will ever need to know about this period of history. I never once made an actual assignment, although I did read books on the subject to them from time to time. We didn't have a culminating medieval feast, and I didn't spend hours and hours fashioning costumes for the children or building scenery and props. They were perfectly content with using their imagination, and filling in with garbage can lids for shields and cardboard tubes for swords. In fact, I believe that they enjoyed the process of creating their own costumes more than they would have enjoyed a teacher-directed activity along these same lines. This reminds me of Charlotte Mason's line, "Boys and girls must have time to invent episodes, carry on adventures, live heroic lives, lay sieges and carry forts, even if the fortress be an old armchair, and in these affairs the elders must neither meddle nor make." (*School Education*, 1907, p. 37) Often, kids can learn more through their own loosely supervised play periods than they can through coerced participation in some "educational" activity that has been devised by an adult.

The reading of the book *The Children's Homer*, which tells the story of the *Iliad* and the *Odyssey*, spawned a similar relaxed unit study. After reading that book, the children got interested in learning about Greek mythology.

We took out a number of books from the library and Laura became especially interested in reading the stories of the gods and goddesses. I realize that a few Christian parents might be surprised to learn that I permitted such a study. However, I believe that children need to learn about such things in order to understand what the Bible is talking about when it mentions the need to forsake idols and false gods. It seems to me that children would have a very difficult time understanding such a prohibition unless they knew a little bit about the way many people thought and worshipped during the Greek and Roman empires.

Anyway, this study of mythology gradually gave way to an interest in other fables, myths, and tall tales. By the time we were leaving the study of false gods behind, the unit study had mutated into a study of Paul Bunyan, Pecos Bill, and John Henry. The children created many short stories, and they wrote several little books of myths and fables on their own.

In addition to such relaxed unit studies, reading good books and biographies of famous people has rounded out our social studies curriculum. There are several excellent sources for such books, including Greenleaf Press, The Elijah Company, and Lifetime Books. For those who want to do a slightly more structured form of unit study, there are also unit study guides available from several authors and companies, including Greenleaf Press.

Studying Science Using Relaxed Units

Relaxed unit studies have also dominated our study of science during the upper elementary years. Some of the topics we have studied in depth include astronomy, archeology, "ichthyology" (the appropriately-named study of fish), and geology. We have learned about birds, insects, and mammals through having pets, bird feeders, and bird baths, and by making a variety of collections. The children have learned about fish by going fishing with Roy and bringing the catch home to identify, discuss, dissect, and eat. As in other areas of the curriculum we usually start with a subject that interests one of us. Then we gradually expand the study until we get tired of it and stop. Often, it will start up again at a later date, when someone else develops an interest in it, or when a new video, magazine article, or book triggers renewed excitement.

In order to make the most of possible learning situations, it is best to have an assortment of science books and nature guides in the home. We have guidebooks about mammals, insects, flowers, fish, weeds, birds, rocks & minerals, and the weather. As a child, I used to save up to buy such guidebooks for myself, and I still have many of these *Golden Nature Guides*, which I purchased for $1.00 apiece back in the fifties. Of course, most have lost their covers by this time, but they are still worthwhile. As money has been available, we have added newer, more complete guidebooks, along with a variety of other resource materials, books, and magazines.

Similar in scope and style to unit studies is something educators refer to as "the project method." We usually have at least one good project going on at our house. These projects have included such things as setting up and maintaining an aquarium; starting seeds indoors; breeding our dog; and creating a nature trail in the woods behind our house. Right now, we are watching a bird build its nest in the fern outside our window, and are trying to figure out how to keep the ants out of our hummingbird feeder. (We learned that a little bit of Avon "Skin So Soft" at the top of the feeder discourages the little critters.) Despite the fact that we don't really think of ourselves as a scientific family, we wind up doing a lot of science-related projects, including gardening, recycling and composting. We currently have a goal of earning enough money at curriculum fairs in 1997 to buy a good camera. Then we plan to start a new project learning about nature photography. Like most of our units or projects, this one began because one person was interested in it. In this case, the person was me! (After all, I'm a student, too!) Laura has also expressed an interest in this area, and it should be a natural for her, since she is both an artist and an outdoors girl. Like most of our other projects, I don't necessarily expect that everybody in the family will be as enthusiastic as the two of us, but I'll bet everybody will get something out of it in their own way.

Elementary Math

As the children reach the upper elementary grades, they become more capable of learning mathematical concepts. Since math is a very logical subject, which builds gradually on information and knowledge that is already in place, it is hard to approach it in the same manner that we approach other areas of the curriculum. For that reason, we typically switch to a textbook approach in the fourth or fifth grade. We have used a variety of texts, including the Saxon series, the Heath textbooks, Abeka, and Bob Jones. Each has its own merits, strengths, and weaknesses. For those who use textbooks, the most important thing is finding a series that works well for a specific child. It is also essential to notice when a textbook approach is not working for an individual. Eventually, we had to switch over to a video format for our oldest daughter, because she simply couldn't understand the math when it was presented solely in written form.

During these years, children are particularly good at learning how to follow rules. For this reason, many children can get right answers in math, even if they have no earthly idea what they are doing. It is always important to keep asking questions to try to determine the degree of actual understanding they possess. Real life experiences must continue to supplement the written curriculum. My children have learned just as much math at my curriculum table, or messing around with their own money, saving, tithing and spending (wisely or foolishly) as they have learned from their textbooks.

Many children this age have difficulty with story problems. The reason often lies in their inability to actually understand the underlying processes. Because they are so good at following rules, they can often get the right answers when the problems are set up for them, but become confused when they are expected to set the problems up themselves. One resource we enjoy using at this age is *Math for Kids*, which is a set of story problems written by children (edited by Susan Richman). Reading these math problems often encourages children to make up their own story problems. Older children might be asked to write such problems for the younger ones. Once they begin to understand the process of writing story problems that deal with simple processes, they can begin to learn how to come to grips with harder problems.

Children this age also often enjoy playing math games or doing related projects. The *Family Math* book from the University of California is one source for such games and projects. I've always liked these projects, because they were created by real mathematicians, rather than third-grade teachers, and it shows. We also like "Muggins" for the upper elementary years, and the older kids have always enjoyed the "Grocery Cart Math" game in Cathy Duffy's "Math Mouse Games." Of course, all math games don't have to come from a curriculum fair, either. One of the best loved math games ever created is "Monopoly."

Teaching Older Children about the Bible

As the children reach the upper elementary years, we usually stop using story books and turn to the real Bible. If children have difficulty understanding the King James Version, I don't mind if they use another one that they can understand. However, I still use the King James version when I am reading to them, or when we are memorizing Scripture. Most decisions like this are probably personal preferences, but the important thing is that children of this age are being introduced to Bible reading as a part of daily life. They are still a little young to study Biblical truths in an abstract manner, but they are never too young to read the stories and learn about the people.

Children who have learned to enjoy reading and who have developed a personal relationship with Jesus will probably be motivated to read the Bible on their own, without a great deal of pressure. One good way to stimulate their interest is to get them their own Bibles with their names embossed in gold on the front. I believe in allowing them to make their own selection, so they can choose one they will want to read.

Art & Music in the Upper Elementary Years

During these years, we continue to use our learning centers for the study of art and music, but we also begin to add in new experiences that reflect the children's greater ability to concentrate and sit still. This is a great age for going to concerts or art galleries. This might also be a good age to study artists or composers in more depth, using Charlotte Mason's technique of having an "artist and composer of the month," and learning more about different time periods in art and music history. Incidentally, for those of you who are basing your art appreciation curriculum on study guides available in the magazines, (such as the art insert in "Homeschooling Today"), be sure to add in more recent periods of art history on your own. The reason that contemporary art is not included in these magazines is not usually that it is less worthwhile, but that it costs more money to pay royalties to use artwork that is less than two hundred years old.

This is also the age I personally prefer to have children begin formal music or art instruction. In my opinion (as a former music teacher), formal lessons in the early years are often counterproductive and are apt to diminish the children's motivation for serious study at a later age. Laura has always enjoyed art and has fooled around with various media for years at our art center. However, she never actually took art lessons until this year, when she reached the age of ten. Because such instruction was postponed until she was really ready to sit still and concentrate, she is more capable of making productive use of the time. She has not been "burned out" by too many early lessons. In the same way, we have postponed private music lessons for our children until they were upper elementary students, although they all played a variety of musical instruments on their own when they were younger.

As always, decisions about when to allow children to take formal lessons outside the house is a very individual thing. In spite of my own hesitancy toward allowing lessons for young children, Steve is currently enrolled in gymnastics. The decision to allow him to take such lessons was based on several factors: his incredible strength (he does 50 push-ups at a time and lifts weights at the age of six); his intense interest; and the fact that he is capable of behaving himself in the group setting even when the other little boys aren't paying attention to the instructor. As with any activity, my husband and I always retain the right to pull the plug if we ever sense that any group, instructor, or experience is having a negative effect on one of our children.

Chapter Eighteen

Working With Young Teens

As you can imagine, I get a lot of mail from homeschooling parents. If I were to divide all of this mail into piles based on the content, the largest pile by far would be composed of those that begin, "I have a twelve or thirteen-year-old who…"

There's something about the middle school years that drives us all crazy. Overnight, it seems like the cooperative, productive children we thought we raised turn into surly, uncommunicative strangers. The boys walk around with chips on their shoulders and the girls retreat into their rooms to cry away their blues. Meanwhile, all of you parents run into your own rooms, turn on your computers, and begin typing letters to Mary Hood or anybody else you think might be able to shed some light on the situation. "Help!" you all cry, "What are we doing wrong? What happened to our precious little children?"

The answer, of course, is that you haven't done anything wrong. That precious little child just isn't a child anymore. He or she has entered a new stage, one that may prove very difficult for all of you. However, it too will pass. Honest. It just might seem like forever for a little while.

The middle school years are usually the hardest for parents to endure, but they are just as difficult for the kids. In order to get through these years without resorting to homicide, you need to understand what is really going on inside those middle school brains and bodies. That's why most of this chapter is devoted to discussing some of the developmental changes that are occurring to kids at this age. The most important change of all, of course, is that they no longer think of themselves as kids at all.

Do you remember when you were in seventh grade? I recall that time of life vividly. I spent most of my waking hours in the company of three girlfriends. We used to call each other the "four musketeers." Those girls meant everything to me. We talked for hours, went for long walks, and discussed everything that was going on in the world. Usually we came up with acceptable solutions in far less time than the United Nations did. In every way, shape, and form, we considered ourselves adults. We believed we were the equals of our parents or possibly their intellectual superiors, since we seemed to know so much more than they did back then! We couldn't understand why they didn't appear to glean anything from our wisdom, which we occasionally tried to share with them to no avail.

Most parents, of course, still tend to view people this age as children. I know my parents did. That's where the problem really begins, with two completely irreconcilable views of the situation. Teens think they are adults; adults think the young teens are still children. Who is really right?

Actually, in my opinion, the teens are closer to the truth. At this age, in more primitive societies, the boys would be passing through rites of puberty and moving into their adult roles. The girls would be getting married soon and starting to raise their own families. Back in Biblical times, there was no prolonged period of adolescence. Many Bible scholars believe that Mary was about fourteen or fifteen when she bore Jesus. The whole concept of the "teenager" was created sometime in the very recent past.

Somewhere, in the depths of their tortured bodies, these young teens sense that they are no longer children. That's why it is so hard for them to deal with the fact that they are usually treated like children in modern American society. The best thing parents can do is to revise their own perception of the situation, and to start thinking of these young people as transitional adults, rather than as some kind of mutant species known as adolescents.

Of course, no matter what the teens may think, they are still lacking wisdom, maturity, and experience. They certainly aren't ready to be thrown out into the world with no parental guidance or boundaries. However, their boundaries need to begin expanding gradually, and they must be treated as if they were intelligent people who are moving ahead towards their adult goals, rather than as if they were a bunch of schoolchildren, confined to their desks for long periods of time each day doing teacher-directed assignments. That is why it is important to begin involving them in the process of setting goals, planning learning experiences, choosing curriculum materials, and keeping their own records. It is also important to gradually help them to find real things to do out in the real world, and to get them out of the house for at least a few hours each week.

In order to work with your teens more effectively during this transitional period, there are four areas of development that you need to understand: cognitive (mental) development, physical development, emotional development, and social development. We'll discuss them in order.

Cognitive Development

Around the age of twelve or thirteen, children pass into a new stage of cognitive development that Jean Piaget labeled "formal, abstract thought." Before this age, children don't really think the same way adults do. (I'm talking about the process of thinking, or "how we think," not the content, or "what we think about.") At this age, the teens are finally able to think in the same manner adults do.

They can now consider abstract possibilities and develop their own opinions about such things as religion, politics, economics, and social issues. As you are undoubtedly aware, they really enjoy forming those opinions and letting us know about it.

This is the age when teens tend to come up to their parents and make statements like, "You know, I've been studying reincarnation and it really makes sense to me," or "I've decided to become a Buddhist," or "It seems to me that Karl Marx had the right idea." I vividly remember the day that I decided that the Peace Corps was an imperialistic tool of the U.S. government and decided to become a Communist. I think it was about a week before I started my first job at the Jewish Old Age Home, received my first paycheck, and discovered that capitalism was the only way to go.

Whatever your young teen believes passionately today will probably be replaced with something just as silly tomorrow. Most parents fly off the handle way too quickly at this stage. That's why I get all the panic-stricken letters, saying, "What happened? Where did we go wrong? I thought we had raised a solid Christian here. How did he suddenly become an atheist?"

The answer, of course, is that these kids aren't really atheists or Buddhists, or anything of the kind. They are just practicing their budding cognitive skills, and starting to think things through for themselves. Without engaging in this kind of thought, they can never make an adult decision to follow Jesus, or decide on a career, or determine whether they are Democrats or Republicans. They need to consider the alternatives for themselves, and will probably pass through several stages before returning to the original values you hope you have adequately instilled.

Your role during this period is twofold. First, you must learn to be a non-judgmental sounding post. These young people need for you to listen to them as they contemplate what they believe about the world around them. They don't need for you to jump on them the minute they open their mouths. I remember my own mother very clearly, sitting in a chair near the window, listening and listening and listening as I poured out my soul about the plight of the poor in Guatemala and why our government was responsible for it. I didn't need a lecture on capitalism or Christianity at that particular moment. All I needed was a willing listener while I spilled out my own theories and wore them into the ground all by myself.

The second thing is to constantly remind your teens, in every way possible, that you still love them, even when you might feel like strangling them. A recent poll revealed that a startling number of young teenagers (around 95%) did not believe that their parents loved them. One reason is that so much of their interaction with their parents at this point is centered on these kinds of "discussions," which rapidly deteriorate into lectures. Too many parents take the kids seriously and overreact, thinking they have to beat some sense into their sons or daughters quickly before they become too old to discipline and are lost forever.

If you love your kids and are willing to tolerate a little nonsense along the way, you're not really going to lose them at all. As with most stages, this one passes away after awhile. Eventually, most teenagers realize that the values and beliefs they were raised with weren't so ridiculous after all. At some point in the not-so-distant future, you may be astonished to find one of them actually asking your opinion about something again!

Individual Variations

Every teenager goes through this stage of questioning while attempting to form his or her own value system, but like everything else, there are individual variations in intensity. Some of them, especially those that are older versions of Dobson's "strong-willed child" may pass through more of a rebellious stage than others. There are also variations in methods. Some young teenagers "think with their mouths," following their parents around all day flapping their gums. My daughter was like that. In some ways, I think I took the place of the three girls who were my constant confidantes. Many girls (and some boys) need human contact in order to discuss things that are on their mind during this stage. Many boys (and some girls) are more "internal." They retreat to their rooms for hours at a time, thinking and ruminating, only to emerge for a few minutes and drop some ridiculous line on the way out the door, leaving their parents with jaws agape, asking, "Where did *that* come from?"

If you have the type of teen who needs to sit alone in his or her room for hours at a time, those hours may not be as unproductive as they look on the surface. The teens just appear to be unproductive because most of the growing is going on inside, where no one else can see. Although you don't want to leave them completely alone at this stage of their lives (after all, they still need guidance, conversation, and protection!), some of them are going to need a lot of "space" in order to complete this stage adequately and move on to the next one.

Of course, you don't need to submerge your own beliefs completely during this stage, either. It is quite natural and permissible for you to occasionally remind your teens what you believe about a particular subject, to express an alternative point of view, or to remind them what the Bible has to say about something. Just don't jump on them too quickly and criticize their beliefs at a time when they feel vulnerable. I think it helps to remember a couple of things when you are talking to your teenagers during this stage:

1. Thirteen year olds are all convinced that they are the center of the universe and that everybody else is focusing on them all of the time. Anything you try to communicate *will* be taken personally, whether you mean it that way or not.
2. Whenever you are doing the talking, all that is happening is that the teenager is waiting for you to stop talking. Although there's no harm in trying to connect once in awhile, it is likely that very little will be accomplished until you stop talking and start listening again.

Physical Development

As most of you have probably noticed, this is an age when there is tremendous physical change taking place in the teenagers' bodies as well. The boys often shoot up half a foot in the span of six months. The girls develop bumps in places that were flat a few days before. Just when they care the most about their outward appearance, they suddenly have to battle oil and zits all over their faces! What a mess! It is quite natural that they feel temporarily out of control in the physical realm. Have you ever thought about how it would feel if you were suddenly six inches taller or your feet suddenly grew to twice the size? Such changes require tremendous adjustments, both physically and emotionally.

Such changes also require a lot of food. When my oldest son was about this age, we started to notice the clandestine disappearance of whole boxes of cookies from the pantry on a daily basis. As an inexperienced parent, I tended to focus on the "stealing" and tried to turn it into a character issue. It wasn't a character issue at all. It was a case of metabolism run amuck. Now that my second son is going through the same stage, I know that three meals a day are just a start at this age. If I don't provide the equivalent of about six meals a day in nutritious food, the slack is going to be taken up with sugar, and you know what that can lead to! The cookies are now kept in less conspicuous places and the specific locations are rotated every week or so. Meanwhile, there are apples and carrots and other snacks available for anyone who might happen to be tearing apart the kitchen looking for sustenance. Eventually, if there are no sugary treats to be found, my son will buckle under the pangs of hunger and eat something that is good for him.

Hormones are also raging out of control at this age, especially in girls. I'm sure most of you mothers remember what it feels like to be pregnant and out of control. Once, long ago, my husband and I were staying in a motel room. Suddenly, a discussion over whether or not we were going to buy a piano turned ugly. I quickly ran into the bathroom, turned on the water faucet and cried for about an hour. I knew a hormonal fit when I felt it coming, and didn't want to inflict it on my husband. Besides, I also realized that ultimately he was going to figure out what was going on, pat me on the back, and say, "I understand. You're just pregnant," and then I was going to have to kill him. In order to avoid premature widowhood, the bathtub was the only possible escape.

Your young daughters are constantly going through this same type of turmoil. That's why almost every discussion that young girls have with their parents culminates in a hysterical retreat to their rooms. When a young teenage boy states that he is now a Buddhist, and is planning to shave his head and go to Tibet, and his parents blow up and ground him for six years, he will probably just turn around and go out to play basketball. A few minutes later, the parents may still be steaming, but the teenager won't even remember the discussion. On the other hand, when a young teenage girl has the same conversation, she will still be crying about it an hour later, even though she can't remember what it was about, either. This leads to the next topic, which is:

Emotional Development

The emotions at this age are often out of control due to these hormonal imbalances. The teens are totally fixated on themselves, their thoughts, their problems, their bodies, their friends, and their self-images, which are often quite low at this point in their lives. The last thing kids this age need is somebody else calling attention to them. I've heard parents talking about their teens right in front of them, pointing out their physical flaws and blemishes, or discussing their good points and their bad points. Kids this age don't need or appreciate any public discussions that call attention to them. They already think everybody else is watching them, anyway. What they need is a good healthy dose of anonymity, especially around strangers. As they feel more competent and confident, they can begin to break out of their shells and enter the adult world, but for awhile, they need a lot of space.

This is a stage when parents should pick their battles carefully. Many teens spend an hour picking out an outfit for church. When they emerge, with pants two sizes too big or a skirt that doesn't match a particular blouse, it is tempting to tell them to go back and change. Unless they are so out of line that you can't help yourself, think again. Try hard to allow them to have some individuality at this point in their lives. Establish those boundaries that you must, and remain consistent in your discipline, but don't sweat the small stuff. There is plenty of big stuff to concentrate on.

Social Development

Most people, (with the notable exception of homeschooling parents) believe that teens this age need to have a large herd of other teens to hang around with in order to be properly socialized. I don't agree. It's true that every teen does have a need for at least one or two good friends during these turbulent years. Everybody needs someone else outside the family in whom to confide. However, larger groups are often actually counterproductive at this age.

During the time our two oldest children were going through this phase, we were temporarily cut off from teenage society. We weren't even members of a church at that time, because we had a baby and a toddler and couldn't find one that didn't think "family night" meant sending them off to another room. Although we missed the fellowship of a church family during those years, we definitely did not miss the negative aspects of church attendance. Now that our third teenager is passing through this stage, we are again back in a rather large, institutional church, complete with a massive "youth program." Sometimes I yearn for the simpler days.

There are reasons why we belong to our church, naturally, or we wouldn't be there. There have been many wonderful things wrought in the lives of our teens. Every one of them has either found Jesus or rededicated his or her life to Him in this church. They have had wonderful missionary opportunities, and have grown tremendously, both spiritually and emotionally, as a result of these experiences. Some of the adult leaders have been wonderful companions to our kids. However, there have also been aspects of the experience that have made me wish fervently that we were alone on a desert island.

Teenagers *always* breed some degree of rebellion when they congregate in crowds. In my opinion, the social needs of teens this age could be served much better by having one or two close friends their own age, and then focusing on involvement in the real, adult world outside their doors. That's one reason I focus so much on volunteer work and apprenticeships at this age. I know that this is sometimes easier said than done. Dan, our current thirteen-year-old, has interests that are harder to meet than those of our older kids. Given that fact and the fact that he tends to be a rather bull-headed "leader" type, it has been almost impossible for me to come up with an apprenticeship activity for him out in the community. In fact, it has been completely impossible so far, because the mere fact that I am the one who thinks of something *automatically* eliminates it, even if it happens to be the very thing he was about to suggest himself. In a case like this, all I can do is to wait until he comes up with something himself. From experience, I know that will happen sooner or later, but it sure does seem like later is a long way off right now.

Courtship vs. Dating

Many people have asked me what our family believes concerning "courtship versus dating." Actually, we haven't had to deal with this issue yet, because it hasn't ever come up. Right now we have a nineteen-year-old son, a sixteen-year-old daughter, and a thirteen-year-old son, and none of them has ever gone out on a date or had anything approaching a real "involvement" with someone of the opposite sex. We never told any of them that they couldn't date. They haven't ever asked! I think the reason for their apparent lack of interest is that they have all been treated like transitional adults, given respect, and helped to find their talents and skills early. They have simply been too focused on their own goals and too busy with their own activities to worry about dating. When teens have such talents and skills, it not only keeps them busy, but it helps them to form a realistic, positive self-image during this crucial time of their lives.

A fourteen-year-old friend recently told me, "When I talk to my homeschooling friends, they are usually discussing the lessons they are taking to get their pilot's license, or the electric guitar they just made, or they are sharing tips on marketing for their home businesses. When I talk to my public school friends, all they talk about is who went out with whom, who bought what at the mall, and what dress they are going to wear to prom. Don't these people have real lives?"

The answer, of course, is *no*. They don't have real lives. They are being treated like children by a society that believes in keeping them cooped up in well-controlled herds, living in climate-controlled schoolroom cages until some magic age when they are suddenly expected to mutate into adults. It doesn't work that way. That's why I believe so strongly in viewing life as a continuum. Young teens are no longer children, and they don't want to be viewed as the "head of the pack." However, they are not yet adults, either, and can't just be turned loose on an unsuspecting society. That's why it so important to understand what they are going through, give them a solid, loving home base, and lead them gradually out into that real world, so they can get their feet wet while still standing on solid ground. (Is that a mixed-up metaphor, or what?)

So Now That We Understand Each Other, What Do We Do?

Figuring out what to do with your young teenagers should be fairly easy, now that you understand them so well, right? *HA*. Living with middle schoolers is *never* easy. However, if you understand their need for some "rites of passage," you do have a tremendous head start.

Most middle schoolers feel a desperate need for change in their lives. In our family, we have had a relaxed approach to education in the lower years. For that reason, our children have typically wanted to switch to a little more structure at this point in their lives. Those who have been raised with textbooks and workbooks might prefer the opposite approach. They may want to be allowed a little more freedom to follow individual interests in a relaxed manner.

This is often a good time to review your own long-range goals for your children and notice any gaps that may have developed. As I've pointed out before, most people look for these gaps way too early. However, by the time young people are twelve or thirteen years old, their own interests and personalities have become fairly well established. At this point, "readiness" is usually no longer an issue. Most are physically, socially, emotionally, and mentally ready to learn just about anything. If something has not been studied yet, it is probably due to a genuine lack of interest or aptitude for a subject. Of course, even adults can suddenly find new interests or aptitudes. As John Holt pointed out in an autobiographical sketch of his own delayed musical career, it is "never too late" to discover new avenues of learning.

As the parent, you must now review your own goals and decide how important particular areas may be for the future development of your children. For example, if a student this age still has difficulty reading, or does not want to sit down and write a simple paragraph, I would view that as a serious deficiency that must be overcome, no matter how difficult or unpleasant the student may view that particular task. On the other hand, if a student this age still has no interest in science, I wouldn't be quite as concerned. I personally don't believe that every single student has to become an expert in the area of science. That is largely dependent on his or her goals. However, I do believe that every student should have a minimal level of knowledge in all the main "school" subjects.

When Ginny was about thirteen, her lack of science interest became obvious. After reviewing my own goals, I decided that she needed to know a little about natural science, a few things about chemistry, and only a few basics in the area of physics. I didn't see the need for her to cover vast amounts of information that she would merely memorize and forget. We did several science-related projects for a couple of years. As the leader of a homeschooler's 4-H group, I planned a trip to a science museum, and followed with a "science fair." Although Ginny wasn't excited about participating, the fact that everybody else was doing a project drew her into the fold. We also made an effort to include her in a few outdoor projects at home, including nature walks, gardening, and making bluebird houses.

As the time approached for her to take the GED, I felt that she was still weak in the area of chemistry, so we took out a chemistry textbook and studied a few things. We went over the periodic table, did two experiments (so she could learn how to conduct and write up an experiment), and studied a little about atoms, molecules, elements, simple compounds, and solutions. We also learned how to balance an equation. This entire chemistry course probably took us a total of twenty hours, done over a period of about two months. Despite the fact that her GED was later waived, I believe this experience acquainted her with the minimal level of chemistry knowledge that is usually required in daily life.

The decision to skip comprehensive science courses was based largely on her individual personality, interests, needs, and goals. My thirteen-year-old son is a completely different person. He isn't sure what he wants to do yet with his life, but he does seem to have a little interest in the area of science. Because of the possibility that he will need more science knowledge down the road, we intend to pursue a more serious study of biology, chemistry, and physics with him. This has led me to establish a homeschooling resource center here in the northern suburbs of Atlanta, complete with a science teacher and biology lab. Kathleen Julicher, the science teacher at the center, laughed at me and suggested there might have been an easier way to meet Dan's need, but I figured that if Dan needed such a resource center, there were probably others out there that needed it even more!

By the way, this is not a situation of "sexism" on my part. Dan doesn't need science just because he is a boy. In fact, my younger daughter, Laura, has several interests, one of which is horses. If she should ever want to be a veterinarian, she will need to be exposed to more science than Ginny did. Ginny plans a career in broadcasting and journalism, and only needs one college science class to graduate. She may change her mind, of course, as many college students do, but I know Ginny pretty well. I doubt highly that she will ever decide to be a mathematician or a scientist. Therefore, I don't believe that a thorough knowledge of upper level science is crucial for her. Besides, if it ever does become necessary, I know from experience that she can pick it up later, when the goal becomes her own. (I taught myself math in my twenties, so I know that all learning does not occur before the age of eighteen.)

As I mentioned earlier, our children have become more structured in their approach to education during the middle school years. This is when I often stepped in with a bit of grammar instruction. One of my teens used *Winston Grammar* and another used the book *Writing for Success*. My daughter, who was already an excellent writer at this point, resisted structured grammar lessons, and I relented. After all, she had already become a published author and earned a 97th percentile on the verbal part of the PSAT.

Finally, when she was sixteen, she came up to me one day and said, "I think it's time I learned what nouns and verbs are." We sat down with a white board and a grammar book, and went over parts of speech and rules for about a week, and that was the end of that. Again, this type of decision requires individual judgement. Ginny's strength has always been writing, so she didn't need much work in that area. Others may need more focus and editorial assistance to develop their talents. On the other hand, Ginny's most serious deficiency was in the area of mathematics. For years, she had resisted math instruction. After taking the PSAT at the age of fourteen, she finally realized her own need to increase her math knowledge in order to get to college some day, and settled down willingly to learn algebra and geometry. In one year, she learned enough to go back and raise her math score from 47th percentile to a level that qualified her for an honor's scholarship to the college of her choice.

Stepping Out Into the Community

During the middle school years, it is also important to help young teenagers find places to work in the community. My two oldest children were volunteers at the public library during these years. Later, Sam spent time as an apprentice is an electronics shop. When Ginny was high school age, she worked as a helper in a first grade classroom in a private school. This taught her, among other things, that she didn't want to be a teacher!

Sometimes it can be difficult finding a spot that will accept young teenagers. If that is the case, it may help if the parent volunteers and brings the teenager along. Often, after the organization has had an opportunity to see a young person in action, they will be more receptive, and the parent can bow out. Volunteer opportunities or apprenticeships may also be found within the homeschooling community itself. Laura has recently found a couple of older homeschooling teens to be her mentors in learning about horses. Another friend of mine recently located a homeschooling father who is in the computer business to help her son learn about the development of web pages.

Whenever a young teen starts volunteering, or accepts a role as an apprentice, he or she should be prepared to begin on the lowest level. Laura hopes to find a volunteer position at a stable one of these days. Eventually, she wants to learn all about horses, but I know what she will be doing to start out! If she is not willing to begin with the dirty work, she won't be able to move up into other areas later on.

Helping Teens Accept Responsibility

In the next chapter, we will be discussing the high school years. By the time your young person is entering high school, he or she should be ready to accept major responsibility for the curriculum: setting personal goals, planning, selecting materials, participating in learning experiences, and keeping records. (Note: I said, "They *should* be ready," not "They *will* be ready.") There are definite individual differences. My oldest son was never ready to accept responsibility in the area of record keeping; hence, no records! I wasn't about to do it for him at that age. My oldest daughter has a system for knowing in which stack important papers are located, but her system looks like chaos to outsiders. My middle son could easily catalogue the entire Library of Congress. They are each unique personalities, and I've learned that you can't change other people when it comes to their basic nature. You can, however, help in small ways to encourage the development of desirable traits. Encouragement is the key, coupled with a lot of prayer. Blowing up rarely accomplishes anything desirable at all.

In order to help your students gradually develop the ability to plan and direct their own education, it is wise to begin during the middle school years. Discuss goal setting with your teenagers, and help them choose the subjects they want to learn. If you feel there is a gap that must be resolved, and you are the one selecting a particular subject or course of study, at least encourage them to participate in the choice of specific materials. When I decided that one of my sons needed to work on his grammar and writing skills, I showed him several possibilities, including *Winston Grammar*, a *Bob Jones* workbook, *Writing for Success,* and *Writing Strands*. Then I let him make his own selection. The goal was mine, and I insisted that he follow through, but he was allowed to take charge of the specific methods and materials himself.

Beginning Homeschooling With Young Teenagers

This last section is addressed to those of you that are pulling young teenagers out of public or private school and starting homeschooling at this age. Good luck. You'll need it!

Okay, I'll try to be a bit more specific. When you are starting to home school a young teen, a lot depends on whose motivation it was to switch gears. If the teenagers themselves asked to come home, you may have willing co-workers. If not, expect resistance.

When working with reluctant teens, try hard to focus on the good points of homeschooling. Emphasize the flexibility and the freedom they will have; the chance they will have to plan their own instruction and take more responsibility for their own lives; and the opportunity they will have to get out into the community or graduate and go to college early. Help them understand that you don't plan to keep them at home all the time. Encourage them to maintain some contact with a few old friends and to find some new ones that are homeschooling. Find places to get them involved out in the community as fast as possible. Above all, don't keep them at home all day long, or they may spend all their time grumbling and missing their fast-paced lives at school.

If possible, it is best to back off a little academically at the start, unless they are motivated on their own. Let them have a little space to get over any dislike of learning that they may have developed at school. Eventually, they will re-discover their own talents and interests. In the meantime, rather than focusing on academics, spend time getting to know each other again on an intimate level. Go to the library together and take out books, tapes, or videos to share. Do things as a family together. Go to some concerts or plays that they would like to see. Allow them to have some time to spend alone, too. Show them that you trust them and give them a healthy dose of respect, even if it seems difficult at the start. When you demonstrate respect for them as individuals, you will eventually win back their respect, too. When they act disrespectful towards others, don't talk about the need for "respecting authority." That just triggers resentment in young people. Talk instead about the need for respecting *all people*, and show them the ways that you are respecting them as individuals.

Ask the teens what they have always wanted to learn, and allow them to follow their own interests as much as possible for awhile. If they have trouble deciding what they want to do, establish some disciplinary ground rules and back off. (Limit their television, telephone, and computer time. Allow boredom to set in. It can be a wonderful motivator.) At the same time, start thinking through your own goals, noticing gaps, and making a few tentative plans, but don't be too quick to start implementing such plans until you have gained a little bit of cooperation.

Above all, don't panic and think everything has to go smoothly right away. Homeschooling is like everything else. You will all need to make adjustments. It might take a little time, but eventually you will be able to establish a good working relationship.

Chapter Nineteen

Preparing for Life Beyond Homeschooling: Age 15+

I went to an urban high school on the fringes of the inner city in Milwaukee. Like many high schools back in the 1960s, we were set up on a "tracking system." This meant that some people were designated as college prep students and others were considered vocational students. The vocational students tended to take easy courses, like family living and art appreciation, and filled in half of their curriculum with subjects that included wood or metal shop, bookkeeping, shorthand, and typing.

Because I had been placed in a "gifted" program when I was in the fifth grade, I was automatically placed in the college prep courses. None of the teachers seemed to notice or care that I was failing most of these courses miserably. Nobody responded when I went to the guidance office and begged to take the secretarial classes. You see, there was one major flaw in their carefully conceived system. Very few people from my high school ever went on to college. Virtually all the boys went off to the military, and the girls had three choices: get married, work in a factory, or get a secretarial job. I knew I didn't want to get married early, and I also knew that there was a good chance I wouldn't be able to afford college. Since I had been working in a bindery every summer during high school, I knew the factory scene was not my cup of tea, either. I desperately wanted to learn secretarial skills so that I could move up in the world, but no one would listen to me.

After becoming convinced that the school would not let me switch from one curriculum to another, I decided to do it on my own. I went out and bought the secretarial books with money earned at my factory job. I learned how to type, keep books, and do shorthand. I took my physics notes in shorthand and then threw them away, since I didn't understand the physics at all. By the time I graduated, I was prepared to go out and get an office job. Although I did wind up going on to college later on, the skills I learned during that time proved invaluable.

This experience taught me something important. If you want a high school student to study and apply himself willingly, you have to connect with that student's desires and goals. By the time students are in high school, *they* should be the ones planning their curriculum. They should be the ones setting goals, working towards these goals, and maintaining their own records. Again, not everyone is created equally in this area, but attaining a degree of independence should always be the ideal and the goal.

Shaking Those Assumptions

In an earlier section of the book, we discussed the importance of identifying assumptions about education and figuring out which ones are still valid and which ones should be eliminated or changed. When high school rolls around, this becomes even more critical. At this point, the assumptions become even harder to discard because they have been written down. It is so easy to be caught up in the system, and assume that four years of English or two years of laboratory science or foreign language are absolutely required for college entrance. By blindly accepting a list of supposed "requirements" for graduation or college entrance, it is very easy to hand the control of our curriculum over to outsiders.

My two oldest children never really took any structured subjects during the high school years. They were both admitted to private colleges and given academic honor's scholarships. Our family has proven that it is not absolutely critical to follow a rigid list of requirements in order to satisfy college admission officials. It is much more important for the students and parents to plan a curriculum that is tailor made for their individual hopes, dreams, interests, and talents.

At the beginning of the ninth grade, the parents and students should sit down together, consider their goals for the future, and plan a basic course of action for the high school years. There are several good resources that may be useful at this time, including *Home School, High School, and Beyond,* by Beverly Adams-Gordon, and Alison McKee's book, *From Homeschool to College and Work: Turning Your Homeschooled Experiences into College and Job Portfolios.* You may also want to listen to my tapes, "Tailoring High School to Your Child's Individual Needs", and "Working with Teens; Preparing for College." Depending on their plans for the future, some students may need a structured curriculum complete with grades, test scores, and credits. Others may not need a rigid structure, and can continue to follow specific interests and develop skills and talents with a minimum of planning and record keeping.

The first step is for the student to attempt to determine whether he or she will be attending a private college, a public university, or a trade school. If the student doesn't have a clear idea of what the future holds, it may be best to plan a middle-of-the-road course, containing all of the "basic subjects," and a few extras in areas of current interest.

Private Christian Colleges

Most four-year Christian liberal arts colleges specify academic requirements in their catalogues, including such things as four years of English, two years of science, three years of social studies, etc. However, when faced with an incoming student who has been homeschooled and who did not follow a traditional curriculum, the vast majority of these schools are happy to relax their requirements as necessary.

These Christian colleges generally look at the individual as a whole. Rather than focusing on what the student has done in the past, they want to determine his or her current academic potential. That's why they rely so much on SAT or ACT test scores. These scores provide standardized assessments of a student's readiness for college work. Those students who plan to attend private Christian colleges must obtain good scores on the verbal and math sections of these tests. One excellent resource for studying for the math section is the Chalk Dust Video Company's "SAT Preparation Series." Those who do not possess high verbal skills need to work on their vocabulary, and obtain some practice with analogies. Educator's Publishing Service has books on these subjects that can be very helpful. Of course, the best way to ensure a high verbal score is to encourage the student to read and write extensively during the high school years.

In addition to SAT scores, these colleges typically want to see samples of the student's communication skills. They often ask for an entrance interview, coupled with an essay or a personal written testimony. The main purpose of such interviews and essays is to determine how well the student can communicate with others. They are also interested in letters of recommendation from adults in the community, and often require such a letter from a pastor or youth pastor who has known the individual for several years.

When our teens applied to colleges, we did not have a formal written transcript. Instead, we submitted a written description of the work we had done in every area of the curriculum over the previous four years. Since Ginny was going away to college at the age of sixteen, we included work she had done beginning at the age of twelve.

Under Georgia law, students are not allowed to take the GED until they are eighteen unless they have a "compelling reason" for taking the test. Usually, most homeschoolers in the state take the SAT first, obtain "conditional admission" from a college, and then ask for permission to take the GED. When we took our materials to the college officials, they not only admitted Ginny, but also waived her GED and gave her a nice honor's scholarship. We had a similar experience when Sam went away to school. The only additional requirement he had was a musical audition.

Don't automatically dismiss the idea of private education because you are afraid that you won't be able to afford it. It is true that private education is more expensive, but the private colleges also have a lot more scholarship money available than the public schools. If you look diligently and begin early enough (at least a year before your student wants to start attending college), you should be able to find a way to make a private school a reality.

Incidentally, there are two types of private schools that may not fit this profile: military academies and those that are secular in nature. In both cases, they may tend to operate more like public universities and have more stringent requirements for entrance.

The reason that the private Christian schools appear to be more receptive to alternate strategies for admission is not that they are easier or lacking in academic quality. They have just recognized that home-educated students usually do very well academically when they get to college, and the admissions officials are always looking for ways to attract and keep good students. Many private colleges are beginning to attend curriculum fairs in an attempt to encourage homeschoolers to apply, and there are even specific homeschooling scholarships available. This is a trend that appears to be spreading as more and more colleges determine than home-educated students are assets to their campuses.

Public Universities

For those students who will attend public universities, the situation is generally reversed. Most of the time, these universities are not nearly as interested in determining current potential as they are in requiring proof of prior accomplishments. Because they tend to be hopelessly bureaucratic, their lists of required subjects are generally set in stone. Any student who comes in with perceived "deficiencies" is apt to be treated as a remedial student and to be given a list of required courses that must be taken without credit. For that reason, students who may be going to public universities need to develop a more traditional curriculum and make sure to keep adequate records. Grades are usually expected, although sometimes "pass-fail" grades may be accepted. There are some public universities who refuse to accept any parent-assigned grades. If your university system falls into this category, you may want to consider going through an accredited correspondence school, such as the American School in Chicago. Often, colleges look at these correspondence schools differently than they look at home schoolers. In our state, for example, attendance at a correspondence school is rated higher than homeschooling for the purpose of handing out "Hope Scholarship" awards.

Even if you want to go to a public university and determine that you need to take traditional courses, there are still ways to make school more interesting and less institutional. There are Supreme Court rulings that clearly state private schools (including home schools) cannot be coerced into using specific curriculum materials or methods. The most standardization that is allowed is in the subject areas covered. In other words, either the government or a college may be able to tell you to take biology, but they can't say exactly what books or experiences you have to use. If a student apprenticed at a marine mammal laboratory, or developed a high-level insect collection, that could be counted as laboratory (hands-on) work just as readily as dissecting worms on a counter. However, when trying to count such alternative experiences, it is very important to keep track of hours and maintain some kind of a journal, so that the work can be substantiated later.

Such alternative experiences can be used in almost any area of the curriculum. Civics can be learned through a legislative apprenticeship. English can consist of reading interesting books and writing real articles for magazines, or even writing and publishing a book. Foreign languages can be learned through inner-city ministries or an overseas stay. One of my young homeschooling friends recently spent six months abroad in Germany, living in a German household and learning the language. She came back with a high degree of fluency, which would probably not have been achieved during the course of a two-year study using textbooks and tapes.

Public universities do not generally have as much scholarship money to give out as private colleges do, so it may not be as critical to receive an extremely high SAT score. However, it is necessary to get a reasonable score in order to ensure entrance. Some public universities also require SAT 2 test scores, which are subject area tests in specific curriculum areas. These tests are rather difficult, so it is best to take them early, (immediately after taking a particular subject in high school), in order to avoid taking remedial classes later. Find out if your system requires them before you sign up.

When considering attendance at secular universities, I hope you take a long and careful look. When our daughter was thinking about attending a nearby secular university, we drove out to the campus and were greeted by a large sign proclaiming the "Gay and Lesbian Dinner Dance" that Friday. It didn't take us long to realize that a public university was not the place for our sixteen-year-old daughter. If students are older, are spiritually mature, and have a definite reason for attending a specific university, they may be able to handle the situation. Just be very careful, and don't forget that our God has a lot of resources. If you submit your decisions to Him, He will provide you with the means to implement whatever course is right for your particular student.

Community Colleges

Sometimes, community colleges may be the first step your student will take into the world of academia. Some community colleges will accept high school students and give them college credits for selected classes. Others will admit young students to various vocational programs. Almost all community colleges have continuing education courses that can be taken by people of different ages for no academic credit.

There are many reasons for considering community college, but there are also cautions that must be considered. A secular community college may have many influences that are anti-Christian in nature. Many of the introductory courses, such as "Sociology 101," are basically attempts to create "open-minded" students, who are prepared to reject the "narrow, old-fashioned" views of their parents.

On the other hand, for a student who needs to attend a secular four-year university, a community college may be a good place to start. For one thing, the bad influences may be less on a two-year campus than a four-year campus. Also, it is usually much easier to obtain admission to a community college. The transcript and test score requirements tend to be less restrictive. After a student has obtained at least thirty credits from a community college (approximately one year of full-time attendance), he or she will probably be treated as a transfer student at a public university and the subject of homeschooling may never come up. For that reason, a community college could be a "back door" into a university system if a student has trouble obtaining admission to a four-year school.

Earning College Credit at Home

Another option for older teenagers is to remain at home and earn college credits through correspondence courses or through CLEP or AP testing programs. Many state university systems have programs that will allow students to earn college credits for work done correspondence-style. In some states, the entire first year's worth of work may be earned in this manner. The University of Nebraska, the University of Florida, and the University of Missouri run popular programs. Admissions criteria for these correspondence programs are often more lenient than their corresponding residence programs.

The AP and CLEP testing programs are administered by the same people that run the SAT testing program. Many colleges will accept up to 30 credits of CLEP credits, so a student may be able to earn an entire year's worth of credits through individual study and examination. AP (advanced placement tests) may also result in college credit, depending on the scores earned. For more information on either of these programs, contact The College Board, Box 886, New York, NY 10101-0886.

Trade Schools & Apprenticeship Programs

For those students who do not want to go to college, there are many other options available. If I had a son or daughter who wanted to be a skilled tradesman, I would not mind at all. Sometimes tradespeople can actually lead richer lives than white-collar workers, both literally and figuratively. However, just because my son or daughter decided not to go to college, their decision would not render all my own goals null and void. In such a case, I would probably not require certain advanced academic classes during high school, but I would still view my own goals as important. For example, I believe that every student needs to become a competent communicator, with skills in reading and writing. I might not require term papers for a high school student who was going to become a carpenter, but I would certainly still make sure he learned how to write business letters and short reports. Similarly, I might not require algebra or trigonometry for someone who wanted to be a secretary, but I would still expect basic math skills in areas such as consumer math, business math, and accounting.

Trade schools often have waiting lists, so look into attendance as early as possible. Most communities have a variety of programs available in such areas as auto mechanics, electronics, and computers. Another possible option might be an apprenticeship. There are two basic types of apprenticeships: formal, structured programs, which may be associated with organizations or labor unions, and informal programs. The formal programs often have strenuous requirements for entrance and a commitment of several years. An example of this would be a program to become a master electrician or plumber. On the other hand, anyone in the community can be approached and asked about the possibility of informal apprenticeships. Sam got his electronics apprenticeship because my husband walked into an electronics shop, saw the work that was going on, and thought, "Sam could do this." He approached the management, and the rest, as they say, is history.

Should Students Home School Through High School?

As with many questions, the answer to this one is dependent on so many specific, personal things that a blanket answer is impossible. If one of our older teens wanted to return to public high school, we would weigh many factors in making a decision. We would look at the specific high school, the individual principal, and the spiritual and academic quality of the faculty. In addition, we would look at our son, and consider his maturity level, his ability to shed adverse influences, and his reasons for wanting to attend. Only after weighing all these factors would we make the decision as to whether or not he should attend.

In many localities, it may be practically impossible to switch back to conventional school in the middle of high school. Many school systems are highly resistant to the idea of accepting homeschooler's credits, unless they have been using an accredited correspondence course. For that reason, I believe that it is imperative to make the decision carefully at the beginning of ninth grade, and then be prepared to stick with it. When my daughter, Ginny, had some inclination to try high school, we made a decision that she would remain a home schooler for two years, and that we would allow her to go away to college early. At the time, I wondered if we would live to regret that decision, but now that she is actually leaving, I know we made the right choice.

Chapter Twenty

Record Keeping & Interfacing with Authorities

A complete discussion of this topic is beyond the scope of this book. If you are interested, you may want to read my booklet entitled, *Relaxed Record Keeping*, which includes sample end-of-year assessment reports and actual log entries from my own journal.

When dealing with authorities, there are several things to keep in mind. First, your own attitude is critical. You need to pray about the people involved before going to meetings, and try hard to avoid appearing confrontational. You need to appear confident and professional yourself, while avoiding viewing the authorities as the "enemy." (Remember that the real enemy is spiritual in nature and can only be overcome through prayer.) Keep in mind that these people have lives of their own. If money were their primary motivation, they wouldn't work in the field of education. They care about children; otherwise they would be in another profession. Most disagreements are due to differences in educational philosophy or religious beliefs. These people do not sit up nights thinking of ways to intimidate you and your children.

Second, remember that first impressions count heavily. Don't arrange to have any interviews in your own home unless you have absolutely no choice. If you have no choice, make sure the house is clean, organized, and free of clutter. Don't take your children along to any interview unless their attendance is mandated by law. If the interview is at home, arrange to have the children someplace else unless the law requires them to attend. If the children must be present, make sure they are well-dressed, well-mannered, and prepared for any interaction they may have with supervisory personnel. Under no circumstances bring an infant or toddler to an interview. You can't act professionally while nursing, changing diapers, or dealing with a temper tantrum. Dress appropriately yourself and have any materials you need organized and kept in a professional satchel or briefcase. If possible, sit at the head of the table, so you appear to be the one in control of the meeting. If not, sit directly opposite the official and look him or her squarely in the eye when discussing issues. Whatever you do, don't walk in looking and acting like a frumpy housewife, with a bunch of papers stuck in a box, a toddler on one hip, and a line of reluctant students walking behind you. If you don't think you can manage to appear professional on your own, hire a babysitter, ask your husband to skip work, and have him deal with the authorities while you sit quietly looking like an extremely competent sidekick.

First impressions also count when evaluators are reading written materials. This includes materials the children have written as well as any assessment reports or journal entries you have written yourself. Unless the law requires that you hand in a written journal, keep your actual journal private. If the law requires a log, keep a separate journal for yourself, where you can feel free to write anything you want, and a separate log for turning in to the authorities. Most states don't expect a great deal of information in such a log. In Pennsylvania, some people get by with a simple check-off system, where they write down the days and hours of instruction, and then check off a list of subjects that were covered .

Make sure that all assessment reports are well written. Have someone knowledgeable check your spelling and grammar if you have any doubts at all about your own writing ability. Much of the impression that the authorities receive is based on your own writing ability, rather than the exact educational experiences you are reporting.

Creating Records

When it comes to record keeping, we are not all created equally. Be sure to come up with a system that will work for you personally. Some people are better at sitting down at a computer once or twice a week, and some people prefer the *Home School Journal*, or a bedside tablet where they keep records just before retiring for the evening. Whatever system you decide to use, do it at the same time every day (or once every week at a particular time) for a month, and the habit will be formed.

My own personal system involves sitting down at the computer every Friday afternoon and writing about the events of the week. I try to include notes on spontaneous conversations, lists of the library books the children are reading, and descriptions of field trips or hands-on activities. I ask the children to keep track of their own library lists and any actual "page numbers" or workbook-type experiences that can be documented easily. They each use a *Home School Journal* (or *High School Home School Journal*) for this purpose. Later, I look at both the children's records and my own journal when writing up my end-of-the-year assessment report.

When it is time for me to write up this report, I print out my computerized journal, and take out the children's records, and try to divide the material up into subjects. For example, if I wrote a notation about working in the garden and discussing the roles of worms, I would include that under "science." A family newspaper started by the kids would come under language arts. A trip to a historical site would be classified as social studies. After I have arranged the various notes into subject categories, I then write an assessment report which includes two or three paragraphs on every subject that is required by law. By doing my report in this manner, I can always come up with something to say in each subject area, even during those years when one of the students has been concentrating heavily on a particular topic. There are always real-life activities in every subject area that can compensate for a lack of structured academics.

When students are high school age, it is helpful to create a portfolio for any subject they take during a particular year. This can be as simple as a file folder which contains such things as an outline of their course work, a personal journal or written report that explains what they did in that subject, letters of recommendation from community people involved in their study, and samples of any written work that was completed. The file could also include photographs, post cards from field trips, and playbills or posters from outside activities. If the student is preparing for the possibility of going to a public university, there should also be a more formal record of hours and grades (percentage grades, letter grades, or pass/fail grades).

There should also be a transcript developed, which will eventually list all subjects taken during the high school years. Keep in mind that those students who are graduating early may want to include seventh or eighth grade work in a "high school" transcript, so they have a record of four years of work whenever they want to apply for admission to college. Also remember that there are alternative ways for completing high school course work. Not all courses have to be driven by textbooks, workbooks, and standard laboratory experiences.

For a complete discussion of how to create end-of-the-year assessments and portfolios, see my booklet, *Relaxed Record Keeping*. Even if you live in a state with fairly lenient laws, it is always a good idea to keep a certain amount of records. In the event you are ever asked to justify your style of education to the authorities, it can be very difficult to remember what you have been doing if you have no records at all to remind you.

"I am come that they might have life, and that they might have it more abundantly." (John 10:10)

Part Four:

Abundant Homeschooling

"I know both how to be abased, and I know how to abound…I can do all things through Christ, which strengtheneth me." (Phil 4:12-13)

"The Lord also will be a refuge for the oppressed, a refuge in time of trouble." (Ps 9:9).\

Chapter Twenty-One

Overcoming Adversity

Homeschooling can seem difficult enough when life is going smoothly, but what happens when things start to go wrong? All of us can expect to experience a degree of adversity at some point in our lives. Some years we may face difficult pregnancies, prolonged illnesses, or deaths in the family. Other years, we may be faced with financial problems, job losses, strikes, or unexpected transfers. It may be difficult to feel confident and joyful during hard times, but there is always an answer to be found. We just need to keep trying and trust that God will provide acceptable solutions.

It is during such periods of crisis that it really helps to have developed a relaxed approach to homeschooling. There is no way that a home in crisis could even begin to emulate the methods of institutional school. However, remaining an effective family is usually possible, even if priorities have to be rearranged for a time.

Awhile back, our family was faced with a prolonged illness and the death of a close grandparent. During that year, it seemed that very little got accomplished on the home front. We were constantly traveling to spend time with the grandparents, since they lived in Mississippi and we lived in Maryland. During that year, we had a hard time maintaining any kind of a home school environment at all. However, the children managed to learn all sorts of lessons from life during that same period, even if the math, social studies, and science had to be put on a back burner.

The following is a reprint from an article that appeared in "The Relaxed Home Schooler" newsletter, which dealt with a similar period in another mother' s life. It described how one family learned to make the best of a bad situation when faced with "one of those years." I thought those of you who missed the article might appreciate the opportunity to share her experience.

But God Had a Different Plan

By Roxane Olmen

In September, we began our fourth year of homeschooling. I thought, "This will be our best. We're going to have all kinds of neat learning experiences and I can finally say to all the skeptics, 'It's working! See what we're accomplishing?'" But God had a different plan.

In early September, my mother-in-law's fragile health took a downward turn and we went to Florida for a visit. We had barely returned home when my mother, who has severe emphysema, broke her right arm, rendering her practically helpless. My daughter and I spent most of October driving the two and a half hours back and forth to give my sister a needed break.

The first month of November found us back in Florida at my mother-in-law's side. We spent time reminiscing, laughing, and looking at old pictures. Unfortunately, she was getting worse and went to be with the Lord two short weeks later. How precious those last two visits are now to all of us.

At Christmas time, my mother began having more health problems, requiring a stay with us. After many tests, surgery was recommended. Cancer cells were found, so more tests were ordered. Thankfully, the results were negative and she could return home in late February. After about a ten-day break, we received a call that my father-in-law had emergency gall bladder surgery. My daughter and I packed up and headed for Florida once again. After a ten day stay, he decided he could handle things himself, so our "medical care mobile" made it back to Georgia.

Have you ever had a year like this? Maybe it was a pregnancy that threw you off your feet for several months, a cross-country move, a devastating illness, or any of a hundred other all-consuming family situations. How did you handle it? What did you *really* do? I'd like to share with you our "story from the road."

Our year was not what we had planned, but it was obviously what God had planned and I'm awfully glad that we were right in the middle of it. I'm so thankful that my children were not locked away in a school room isolated from the caring, the sharing, the waiting, the crying, the serving. They were being submerged in real life, which taught them lessons I may never be able to assess.

Where did homeschooling fit into a year like this? To us, this *was* homeschooling! It might not have been books or math, but it was a lifestyle of learning in the context of what God was doing in our family. Books were laid aside as more important matters were attended to. There was so much time spent in caring for relatives that there was little or none left for formal lessons of any kind.

Days were filled with doctor visits, pharmacy trips, a back rub here and a game of Scrabble there. I kept saying, "We have to get something done that remotely resembles school work." But there were weeks when that simply was not possible. I spent a lot of time in a panic. I would say, " When things get back to normal in a week or two, we'll do..." And then someone else would need us.

I spent a lot of time praying about the whole thing, asking the Father to make something beautiful out of our crazy, mixed-up year, and an answer began to take shape. I've often said that I believe in learning all the time. If that's true, the children must be continuing to learn in the midst of these difficult times!

I decided to make some simple observations. What were we really doing during some of these crisis times? For one thing, we watched movies. "Apollo 13" caused us to talk about how weight affects the trajectory of a rocket. "Gone with the Wind" brought discussions of antebellum etiquette and Civil War sufferings.

Discussions with relatives were also learning experiences. Looking at old pictures of Grandma and Grandpa ignited stories of World War II and war-time shortages. The children sang songs and learned about country living with Aunt Kathy. They climbed trees, roasted marshmallows over a bonfire, and watched a cat have her kittens. They made crafts and collages, drew pictures, and read magazines. My daughter taught herself how to roller-skate, made a kite, played Password, made Origami creations, and discovered the joys of reading old "Uncle Remus" stories. She listened to countless stories about Papa's work as an inventor, a college professor, and an active Gideon. My mother regaled them with stories of growing up in a large family. Last, but not least, my children had plenty of time to spend just sitting and thinking, being still. (Now there's a skill we don't hear a lot about at curriculum fairs.) My teenage son also stayed with Dad for ten days while we were away and learned to care for the house entirely by himself, cooking a full meal every night, washing dishes, and doing laundry.

It is so easy to get the notion that the only time our children will learn anything is when we are in control and it is a planned educational activity. When we realize that we are not in control, we are forced to re-examine long-held beliefs. What I found was that all of my children's learning did not depend on me. Hopefully, my children have learned the most important lesson of all. God is in control, and we can rest in Him when life seems to get out of whack. If you find yourself in a year when events beyond your control throw your home school into a tailspin, remember to rest in the One Who is really in control. It could turn out to be your finest hour.

P. S. We ended our school year with my mother having a biopsy and my husband having minor surgery. And the learning goes on...

By Roxane Olmen

From my own experience with a similar year, I'd like to add one or two comments. For me, it has been absolutely critical to review my long-range goals once a month or so during such times of hardship. For one thing, reviewing those goals usually reassures me that something good has already been accomplished, and that all will not be lost if a year slips by without much forward motion. Second, I can usually pinpoint one or two areas that are causing me the most distress.

For example, if I had a six-year-old who was just in the throes of learning to read when chaos hit, I would get very frustrated if I wasn't able to help him out with his reading at least once a day. On the other hand, I would also recognize that math, science, and social studies wouldn't suffer that much if they had to be postponed for a year or so. If one of my older children was just about to take the SAT, I would know that it wasn't a good year to take a complete break from math work, but I might be willing to forget about the term paper we had been planning. My long-range goals would therefore help me to set priorities for the short periods of time that were actually available for academic work.

When smaller children are around, adversity can really threaten the sanity of a homeschooling mom. My friend, Roxane, had a tough enough time coping with the stresses of her crazy, mixed-up year. How would she have managed if she also had a couple of toddlers or nursing babies to add to the confusion? When faced with such a situation, it becomes critical to remember the main focus of motherhood: to raise children who are safe, physically healthy, emotionally balanced, and spiritually grounded. You may need to overlook virtually everything else, and temporarily scrap much of the housework and all of the schoolwork in favor of peace and harmony.

When older students are involved, it is often easier to set aside a couple of hours a day for them to spend on academics, as long as you are willing to trust them with their own planning and record keeping. If you believe that you must constantly get involved with their educational pursuits, planning and checking papers, grading and maintaining adequate records, you probably won't be able to do it. On the other hand, if you can trust them to adequately plan and execute their own learning experiences, you can probably manage to carve out some time for them to accomplish things on their own. Older students can also be expected to contribute to the workload around the home during off hours. Their realization that free time might be limited during crises is a part of learning about the way the real world operates.

At times of crisis, everybody must pull together and make sacrifices. That might involve giving up individual activities, such as gymnastics or baseball, until the time of chaos has passed. Any actual free time should be spent doing things that everybody in the family can enjoy, including the mother. Otherwise, chauffeuring responsibilities might wind up being the straw that breaks the proverbial back.

Dealing With Chronic Problems

What happens if your crisis turns into a chronic problem, one that doesn't go away after a year has passed? I have known homeschooling mothers that must operate out of a wheelchair, or cope with life on a single leg, following cancer and the amputation of the other limb. A blind woman once came up to our booth at a curriculum fair, with four children in tow, selecting her curriculum by asking her children to explain each item on the table. Others have had to live with an elderly parent on a regular basis and provide intensive care. Still others have had children with special needs. One homeschooling father recently had an auto accident, was paralyzed, and lost his job. For those of us with simpler lives, it is hard to visualize what home schooling must be like under such difficult circumstances.

When faced with such problems some people might be tempted to just "pack it in" and put the children back in school. While that might wind up being the only acceptable alternative in some cases, it's important to think carefully before succumbing to the temptation to find a quick fix.

One of the good things about homeschooling is always the flexibility. Placing the children back in school may present you with a whole new set of difficulties. You will lose control of your own schedule. You will probably need to get up early and stay up late helping with homework. You might want to ask yourself if it is worth it in the long run. What is it that you think the children will be gaining that is so important? Perhaps they may have more opportunity to learn certain academic matters in school, but they may also wind up losing ground when it comes to character training.

When making difficult decisions, it is again helpful to review your long-range goals. Keeping in mind that you have twenty-four hours a day, 365 days a year, to accomplish your goals, you can recognize that slow growth may not be all that bad in the long run. If a student has to take several weeks off from academic work at a time, he may still get just as much done in the long run as a student who is sitting in class six hours a day, wasting much of that time in non-academic pursuits. For one thing, homeschoolers have the entire summer to catch up if necessary, whereas typical school students spend most of their summers forgetting information and much of the fall reviewing what they have forgotten.

Searching for Support

The most important thing to do in difficult circumstances is to surround yourself with an effective support team. This team might include your husband, your older children, neighbors, church friends, or members of your extended family. Don't be reluctant to ask for help when you need it. That's what friends and relatives are there for.

When there is little support in the immediate area, it is also helpful to look for larger organizations that might be able to provide you with long-distance support. For example, there is the NATTHAN organization for parents who are homeschooling special needs children. If you can't locate any help at all from people, near or far, remember that you can always turn to God. He will never let you down, and He's always just a prayer away.

Reliance on God

In times of trouble, even reluctant people often turn to God for assistance. If you already know Him and are on intimate terms with Him during your good times, you will certainly be able to count on His help during the tough years. Even in the midst of a crisis, it is very important to carve out some time to spend quietly with the Lord each day, renewing your strength and asking for specific help with problems that arise. Remember to live in "day-tight" compartments at times like this. Don't allow your mind to wander back to the days when your life was simpler, and don't allow your imagination to conjure up images of what the future might hold for your family. Just concentrate on living each day, setting and working towards a few realistic goals. Rely on God's strength to get you through each day successfully, one day at a time. Fill your mind with appropriate Bible verses, such as the following:

When taking a break:

"I laid me down and slept. I awoke, for the Lord sustained me." Ps 3:5).

"Be ye transformed by the renewing of your mind." (Romans 12:2)

"Peace I leave with you, my peace I give unto you. Not as the world giveth, give I onto you. Let not your heart be troubled, neither let it be afraid" (John 14:27)

When feeling overwhelmed:

"I can do all things through Christ which strengtheneth me." (Phil. 4:13)

"I am the Lord, the God of all mankind. Is there anything too hard for me?" (Jer 32:27)

"Being confident of this very thing, that he which hath begun a good work in you will perform it until the day of Jesus Christ." (Phil 1:6))

When questioning the reason for the turmoil:

"All things work together for good to them that love God." (Romans 8:28)

"We glory in tribulations also, knowing that tribulation worketh patience, and patience, experience, and experience, hope." (Romans 5:3-4).

Chapter Twenty-Two

Overcoming Spiritual Attacks

"Put on the whole armour of God, that ye may be able to stand against the wiles of the devil." (Eph 6:11)

In *Onto the Yellow School Bus and Through the Gates of Hell*, I discussed spiritual warfare. Most home schoolers recognize that the powers of Satan have been running amuck in the public school system since God was kicked out of the decision-making process. While I don't intend to judge those parents whose children remain in public school, I hope that they understand that constant vigilance in prayer is necessary to protect young children in that situation. The children themselves cannot possibly be mature enough to stand alone as Christian soldiers in the middle of a major battle. Mature Christian school teachers, principals, and parents can be "salt and light" in the public school. Even some older teens may be able to serve in this capacity. Immature young children, left alone without the protection of their parents, are much more likely to be influenced by the negative forces they encounter than to influence others for the Kingdom of God.

One thing is certain. Satan doesn't want you to teach your children at home. He doesn't want you to remove them from the public sphere, and he doesn't want you to center their education on the teachings of Christ. He is bound to attack you or your loved ones if given any opportunity to do so.

Some Christians tend to see demons sitting behind every rock. In my opinion, it is not scriptural to blame every personality defect, every temper tantrum, or every family calamity on demonic forces. If you are scraping by financially, it might be because you made bad decisions somewhere along the way, or it might be God's plan to make you stronger through overcoming adversity. If you are sick, it might be because you slept with the window open, forgot to wash your hands after you worked at the church bazaar, or are just plain allergic to goldenrod. Every bad experience does not come directly from the hand of Satan. It is necessary to be discerning, and recognize spiritual attacks when they do come without blaming demons for every single thing that goes wrong in your family.

There are definite times and situations when spiritual attack is most likely. I don't claim to be an expert on this subject, but I have had some experience recognizing and warding off personal attacks on our family. I also believe that God has given me a certain measure of wisdom relating to such attacks, and I want to share it with you as much as possible. The following situations should be watched carefully:

1. Any time there is spiritual dissension in the family. In our family, my mother was a Christian and my father dabbled in "New Age" philosophies. This set us up for constant spiritual attack and conflicts.

2. Any time any family member has "cracks" in his or her personal armor, whether through unconfessed sin, lack of forgiveness, or playing around with occultic influences (i.e., thinking too much about UFOs or reincarnation; playing with ouija boards; and dabbling in such things as tarot cards, astrology, or automatic writing).

3. Any time a family member has just committed his or her life to Christ, or stands up publicly for the first time to give a testimony. Satan often

goes after "Baby Christians," hoping to lure them back to his side before they get strong enough to stand up to him forever.

4. Any time any family member is going through tremendous spiritual growth, especially if that growth has not yet resulted in a complete commitment to the Lord. Whenever somebody starts reading the Bible regularly, praying, or engaging in any spiritual activity they have not been doing before, it is *crucial* that other family members pray for their safety during this period of spiritual growth.

5. Any time anyone is reading or studying about spiritual warfare, including reading this book. Satan doesn't like it when he knows he is being exposed. That's why I am stopping writing right now to pray for your safety while you are reading this. (And I added another prayer that your kids will find something quiet to do so that you can have a few minutes to yourself.)

6. Any time anyone in the family is undertaking a special assignment that may lead to advances in God's kingdom. At times like mission trips, or the beginning of a new Christian-based business, people are often especially vulnerable to Satanic attacks. Our three oldest children recently returned from a mission trip to Minnesota. They had to deal with automobile problems, a car crash that landed Sam and one of the adult leaders in the hospital, and a near miss with a tornado. There were just too many problems to be total coincidences. However, the prayers of the church members back at home ensured that all of the members of the mission group eventually returned unscathed.

The most massive demonic onslaught that our family ever withstood occurred during the publishing of *Onto the Yellow School Bus and Through the Gates of Hell*. During that time, Satan used my own relatives and close friends to try to force me to take my mind off the book and stop the printing process. He tried to destroy the good name of our family. He attempted to destroy our relationship with several close relatives. He tried to use sickness and bad weather to sabotage speaking tours when I was talking about spiritual warfare. However, God watched over us during that entire period. Despite having a variety of seemingly impossible situations to wade through, we eventually came out victorious on every front.

In order for you to be victorious in such circumstances, too, it is absolutely imperative that you learn to recognize spiritual attacks and to understand what they are, what their purpose is, and where they originate. You must also learn how to combat them in the name of the Lord.

Such attacks are simply attempts by Satan and his demons to discourage Christians who are working to bring about the Kingdom of God and to prevent non-believers from becoming Christians. The purpose of such attacks is simple. They are motivated by hate, and represent Satan's desire to kill and destroy everybody on earth. He knows he is doomed himself, and wants to bring as many others down with him as possible.

Combating spiritual attacks is not easy. In fact, it is impossible when you try to defend yourself on your own strength. Satan and his demons are far more powerful than you are. However, God's power is much greater than Satan's power, and it is there for you to tap into any time you want. All you have to do is to recognize what is going on, to "bind" the demons in the name of Jesus, and to ask God to fight your battle for you. It really doesn't have to be a scary process. However, in order to be adequately prepared, you must make sure that your "spiritual armor" is fully in place.

In Ephesians, we read:

> *Put on the whole armour of God, that ye may be able to stand against the wiles of the devil. For we wrestle not against flesh and blood, but against principalities, against powers, against the rulers of the darkness of this world, against spiritual wickedness in high places.*
>
> *Wherefore take unto you the whole armour of God, that ye may be able to withstand in the evil day, and having done all, to stand. Stand therefore, having your loins girt about with truth and having on the breastplate of righteousness; and your feet shod with the preparation of the gospel of peace; Above all taking the shield of faith, wherewith ye shall be able to quench all the fiery darts of the wicked. And take the helmet of salvation, and the sword of the Spirit, which is the word of God."*
> *(Eph 6:11-17)*

Note especially the comment about the breastplate of righteousness. If that breastplate has a crack in it, due to unforgiveness, unconfessed sin, lack of submission to Christ, or anything else, your vulnerable heart area will be open to attack. That's why the first step in fending off spiritual attack is to make sure your own heart is right with God. Once you are fully convinced that you are ready, take up the sword of the Word of God, and believe what it says: "We are more than conquerors through Him that loved us." (Romans 8:37) Picture a "conqueror" ... someone like Alexander the Great, maybe. We are supposed to be stronger and tougher than that! Just imagine! We have absolutely no reason to fear the forces of Satan, either in our own lives or those of our children.

It is important that mature Christians also surround their children with constant prayers of protection. That is what I urge parents to do when they have students in public school. It is just as important for parents of children who are being home-educated. Every time my teenagers get in a car, I ask the Lord to send a few angels to surround them. A couple of months ago, a deer jumped into the road just ahead of Sam. The car swerved into the other line of traffic, hit several trees, and skidded down an embankment. It was completely ruined, but he walked away without a scratch. Without our constant prayers for protection, an incident like that might have had a different outcome.

It is also important to monitor the influences that are allowed into your family, so that no breaks can be found in anyone's spiritual armor. Any occultic ideas or influences must be carefully weeded out and disavowed, unless a subject is being studied in a scholarly manner under the guidance of mature Christians. This includes things like the study of weird phenomena (i.e., the Bermuda triangle, the Loch Ness monster, the Roswell incident, etc.), and the study of such topics as eastern religions, reincarnation, and ESP. It also includes such practices as celebrating Halloween, watching "cute" television shows about witches or cartoons that have their roots in the occult, listening to certain types of non-Christian music, and playing fantasy games, especially dangerous ones like "Dungeons and Dragons."

Some of this might sound a little weird or unnecessary to those of you who have never experienced spiritual attack. As a youngster growing up in a split household, reading about God as well as reading about and performing occultic practices, I know what I'm talking about. One time, I was lying in my bed trying to have an out-of-body experience (or "levitate") when a force threw me to the floor and I had to struggle to keep it from taking me over completely. That scared me, but it didn't completely stop me from a fascination with weird things at the time.

In my book on spiritual warfare, *Onto the Yellow School Bus and Through the Gates of* Hell, I gave a complete account of the struggles I went through as a young mother. It seemed that the closer I got to a genuine belief in God, the more Satan tried to attack. I had so many rips in my own armor at the time that it was like going into battle protected by Saran Wrap.

Eventually, I had a vision, where I saw myself standing in a doorway. On one side was a bright light. The other side was inky darkness. I knew that I had been standing with one foot in each world, and it was time to make a decision. As I pulled my foot into the light, I knew that my life would never be the same.

Since that time, spiritual attacks come from time to time, but now I recognize them for what they are. They have no more power to hold me down. However, the stronger I become, the more Satan seems to try to go after my children. He will always target the weaker members of the family. That's why I still have to stay on my toes and pray away any negative influences before they have a chance to get a foothold in our lives.

"Bring ye all the tithes into the storehouse, that there may be meat in mine house, and prove me now herewith, saith the Lord of hosts, if I will not open you the windows of heaven and pour you out a blessing that there shall not be room enough to receive it." (Malachi 3:10)

Chapter Twenty-Three

Overcoming Financial Difficulties

About four years ago, our family launched "The Relaxed Home Schooler Newsletter." At first, it was a completely free publication that was given away at curriculum fairs. Eventually, the mailing list became too long, because it wound up on the internet somehow and was advertised as a free publication in several magazines. The last free issue wound up costing us over $2,000 to print and mail. At that point, we were faced with three possible choices: stop publishing the newsletter completely, switch to a magazine format, or start charging for an expanded version of the newsletter. We opted for the latter. Since that time, God has blessed our efforts, and it has continued to flourish in this new format.

Yet one thing puzzles me. At the time of this writing, the newsletter costs only $6.00 per year. That doesn't sound like a lot of money. Yet, in order to make the publication available to everyone, there is also an option to request a free subscription for those who state that they really can't afford it. Over a hundred homeschooling mothers have done that in the past year.

It's not that I begrudge any of you a free subscription. Far from it. If we are being blessed, I'm very willing to share that blessing with all of you. I also know from experience how difficult it can be to stretch a paycheck when only one parent is able to work outside the home. Yet I can't help but wonder. If we are all doing our best to do God's will for our families, and if His preferred plan is for the father to work and the mother to stay at home with the kids, why has it become almost impossible to make ends meet on one income these days?

Oh, I know all the standard answers. I studied economics in college, but I also know all about God's infinite capacity to bless His people. I don't mean to sound like I have all the answers, and I certainly don't mean to judge any of you. I know how difficult it can be to make a paycheck stretch these days, and I also know that many of the suggestions that I'm going to make in this chapter are "old hat" to many of you. I feel a little uncomfortable sounding like I'm preaching. Still, I can't shake the feeling that a lot of financial situations could be vastly improved by the consistent application of three or four simple principles concerning finance.

The first of these principles is an understanding of God's abundance. A few homeschoolers actually seem to take pride in living a life of scarcity, but that is not what God promises in the Bible. In Malachi, we read, "Bring ye all the tithes into the storehouse, that there may be meat in mine house, and prove me now herewith, saith the Lord of hosts, if I will not open you the windows of heaven and pour you out a blessing that there shall not be room enough to receive it." (Malachi 3:10)

Some Christians seem to believe that it is unbiblical to ask for or expect abundance or riches. It is true that a desire for riches in excess of actual need is not healthy. Jesus warns about the dangers associated with idolizing money and turning it into a God. He told one young man that he had to give all his riches away to the poor in order to come and follow Him. That was probably because He knew that this particular person was hung up on money at the time.

Taking a vow of poverty wasn't meant as a standard for all of us to follow, however. Many of the great Bible characters, like Abraham, Job, and Solomon, were blessed with great riches. For most committed Christians, abundance itself is not wicked, and will not hinder our ability to live a decent life here on earth or to get to Heaven someday. Jesus always looks at the state of our hearts. He doesn't look to see how much money we have. He wants to know where we have laid up our treasure. (Matt 6:21) There is a difference. Jesus is also interested in observing what we do with the resources we have been given. When God "loans" us talents or worldly goods, we are expected to make appropriate use of them (Matt 25:14-29).

A few homeschooling mothers seem to "thrive" on a condition of lack. They actually become prideful about their ability to clip coupons, shop at day-old bread stores, and buy used curriculum year after year. Naturally, when that is all that can be afforded, they have to do what they have to do. In many cases, couponing and resource sharing are the only ways for mothers of little children to stay at home. In such cases, their efforts *should* be applauded (but not by them!) However, this type of lifestyle should always be viewed as temporary. It should never be accepted as a permanent condition. Both parents need to make plans that anticipate future abundance, rather than anticipating a continued state of semi-poverty and justifying a lack of planning by patting themselves on the back for their frugality and citing their "trust in God." A true trust in God includes a knowledge that He has no intention of letting His saints wallow in poverty, unless they have actually taken such a vow for spiritual purposes.

Of course, very few homeschoolers would say that they actually desire a life full of financial trouble. Most would say that they crave abundance, but few are able to get over the worldly belief that a family simply can't make it happen on a single income anymore.

To begin experiencing a life of financial abundance, the first thing you need to do is to stop thinking and planning for scarcity. You need to start thinking, planning, praying, and setting goals that will lead to financial prosperity, instead. As all the "success books" state, it is always best to come up with goals that are realistic, personally important, written down, and reviewed on a daily basis. When it comes to finances, it is also important that the mother and father act as a unified team.

Once you have some dreams, some realistic goals, and a few beginning plans, you need to purposefully unclasp your fists. God can't pour prosperity into your hands unless they are open and ready to receive it. That means that your hands must first be open when it comes to giving. The statement in Malachi about "overflowing" abundance is closely tied to the practice of tithing and giving to the Lord's business. No matter how "strapped" you may be for funds, your first priority should always be giving God back what belongs to Him, the first 10% of your fruit. If this worries you, just try it for awhile and see what happens. I have learned that you simply cannot outgive God. Whatever you give to Him and to His work will come back multiplied. Sometimes it happens immediately and sometimes you have to wait awhile, but eventually the laws of God's kingdom will always come through.

In my opinion, questions such as," Do I tithe off my gross or my net?", or "Do I give to the local church or to another charity?" miss the main point. God loves a cheerful giver. He isn't an accountant. He is looking for the proper attitude in your heart.

Another important step toward financial prosperity is to "bind" any efforts on the part of Satan and his demons to hold you down in poverty. There is such a thing as a "spirit" of poverty that can attach itself to an individual or family. Tell this spirit to go away and find something else to do. Inform him that you intend to live a life of prosperity here on earth and in Heaven!

From that point on, of course, there are clear Biblical laws that relate to the handling of finances. The most important, in my opinion, is to avoid going into debt. I have heard a well-meaning preacher state that this prohibition against going into debt does not apply to house mortgages, which are simply "budgeted expenses," but I don't see that anywhere in the Bible. When and if an economic collapse comes, those with mortgages they can't repay will be in serious danger of losing everything. That is especially true if the mortgage contains a "surety" clause, which is fairly standard practice today. This clause gives the lending institution the right to collect from all of your other personal assets if you can't repay the mortgage note. In other words, if the economy suddenly crashes and your $100,000 house is suddenly worth $25,000 and you still owe $75,000, the bank can seize your house, take your equity, and then go after all your other assets. They can even garnish your husband's wages, assuming he is still employed. In short, unless the mortgage can be paid back, the bank can take everything you own and force you into bankruptcy. That's why people like Larry Burkett have been warning Christians that debt reduction should always be the most important element in any plan to improve a person's financial situation. (Contrary to what the world believes, debt reduction is not the same thing as debt consolidation, where you take all your credit card debt, refinance it with an equity home loan, and put your home into jeopardy even more.) If the only way to eliminate a mortgage with a surety clause is to sell your house and rent for awhile, I'd strongly encourage you to consider that option.

A few of my friends scoff when I talk to them about such things and accuse me of a lack of trust in God. I think that it's wonderful to trust God with the future, but I don't believe He has any responsibility for bailing out people who are disregarding His laws. It is totally scriptural to prepare for a possible economic collapse, as long as you recognize God's sovereignty, and seek His continued help.

Without Joseph's preparation, the people of Egypt and Israel would have starved during the seven lean years. God spoke to Joseph about the need to prepare and Joseph listened to Him. If God is doing His best to speak to you through the work of people like Larry Burkett, and you are not willing to listen, He may not be willing to bail you out when the crisis hits.

In the Bible, the "year of jubilee" took place every fifty years. At that time, all debts were repaid and everybody started out again from scratch. In modern times, since this law is no longer followed, economic cycles have developed that practically ensure a major depression every sixty years or so. In 1997, America is well past the sixty-year mark. The only reason I can imagine that our economy has not yet collapsed is because God is holding it up for a purpose. Perhaps He wants the resources of America available for a massive evangelistic push as we reach the year 2000. Perhaps He is giving some of us a little more time to get our affairs in order. Whatever His reasons, He won't stop the natural forces forever. Unless the Lord returns within the next few years, the economy *will* have a major upset sometime soon. It's time to start preparing now.

Starting a Relaxed Home Business

In 1990, I finished my Ph.D. in education. Up to that time, I had found a nice balance in my life, enjoying my time with my small children while having an occasional outlet for pursuing my own interests. Each semester for the past ten years, I had taken one or two classes at a time. Suddenly, I found myself without any place to go at night. I started to get depressed and play a lot of Packman.

Of course, I could have gone out and taken a high-powered professional job, but I didn't want to leave my children or stop homeschooling. I knew that I had a lot to share with other mothers, but I tried to write a few pieces for the magazines and had very little luck. I wrote one major book on educational philosophy and submitted it to one publisher after another, with the same result. It seemed like all I was doing was spinning my wheels.

Finally, one day Roy came in while I was playing Packman, and said something simple like, "Nice pastime for someone with a Ph.D." I gave him a woebegone look and said, "There's nothing else I can do." He gave me a sidewise look and said, "Oh yes, there is."

That might not sound like an earthshattering comment, but somehow he got through to me that night. Suddenly I decided it was time to get moving again. I began to gather up all the information I knew about homeschooling and created a small packet of information, which I cleverly named, "Information Packet on Home Schooling." Then I placed a $300 ad in "Mother Earth News," saying something like, "You can teach your children at home. Everything you need to know how to make it a success." Then I sat back and waited for the money to roll in...and waited...and waited. Finally I decided that I had chosen the wrong publication and blew another $250 putting a similar ad in the LaLeche League magazine. Again I waited. Again I wound up losing money.

Sometimes it is necessary to fail a few times before coming up with an idea that will really work. Eventually, I began sending letters to public libraries advertising this "packet of information" and started to make a few sales. Then I improved the packet, renamed it *The Home Schooling Resource Guide & Directory of Organizations*, and began learning how to market the booklet more effectively. At the same time, I began to seek places to speak to home-schooling mothers. I still wasn't making much money, but at least I was able to pay back the advertising money I had borrowed from our family funds, so I didn't feel like a complete failure any more.

The next endeavor was to take the information I had gathered during my dissertation research and use it to help other homeschooling parents understand their own beliefs about education. I created my *Countdown to Consistency* workshop and published a workbook to go with it. This time, I risked $1,000 of our family funds to get the workbook printed. Despite a fair amount of success with that workshop, I still have half of those workbooks downstairs in my basement. It took me about two years to repay the family bank that time. Success doesn't happen overnight!

The turning point came in 1993, when I wrote *The Relaxed Home School*. This time, I didn't waste any time looking for another publisher. Instead, I bought a book by Judith Apelbaum, entitled, *How to Get Happily Published*, and published the book myself. Her book taught me just enough about copyrights and ISBN numbers to locate the appropriate places to call and sound like a moron. That's one of the keys to starting a successful business without a business degree. You have to be willing to sound stupid, ask a million questions, and be laughed at…a *lot!*

During the first three years, I didn't take any money out of the business to spend on anything for the family. Any profits I made went right back into the business to purchase additional stock and equipment, such as file cabinets and computer hardware, and a new van. (Actually, my husband and I went "halfsies" on the new van. Profits haven't been *that* phenomenal!) Our lifestyle has not changed much because of the business, but I have also not "failed," which happens to 90% of new businesses during the first three years. One of the main reasons that I didn't fail was that I didn't borrow any money from anyone outside the family, and I didn't rent quarters outside the home. I also didn't try to start out too large, but instead began very small and gradually built things up as resources became available.

Now, at the four-year-mark, the business is ready to take a calculated risk. I'm sinking all my savings into an attempt to create a home-schooling resource center. The center may take off. If so, we're hoping my husband may be able to retire early and come join me in the business in another year or so. On the other hand, the center may fail. However, I know that a failure couldn't sink us personally, since I have enough back-up savings to cover any potential losses the first year.

Based on my own experiences in starting and running a business, I'd like to share a few pointers for those of you who are tempted to follow in my footsteps:

To begin with, there are good and bad reasons for starting a home business. One really bad reason is to give your children a way to learn about work responsibilities in the context of the home. This is recommended by several men in the home-schooling arena. Trust me. They have never tried to juggle mothering, homeschooling, and running a home business. It may sound like a good idea on paper, but the children are apt to lose more than they gain during the first few years. When mothers tell me they are starting a business to help their children learn math skills, it reminds me of my own abortive attempt to earn money delivering phone books when Sam and Ginny were small. I had this picture in my mind of the three of us walking down the street with a little red wagon, happily taking turns running up to the front porches delivering books. In reality, I wound up with two hungry children sitting in the car amidst hundreds of phone books, while I ran up to the fourth floor of an office building with ten books. The man up there looked at me and said, "But I ordered 100 books." At that point, I ran home with my tail between my legs and asked Roy if he would mind returning a thousand phone books for me the following morning on the way to work.

Another really bad reason to start a business of your own is to "earn a little money of your own." One thing Roy and I have discovered over the course of a twenty-year-marriage is that the attitude of my money...your money is absolutely ruinous in a marriage relationship. Get it through your head that *all* the money your husband makes is *your* money, too. Then prove you are capable of handing it jointly in an intelligent, fair manner.

On the other hand, there are several good reasons to start a business. They include:

- ✓ Because your smallest child is at least five years of age, you have a couple of hours a day to devote to a business, and you'd just like to give it a try.
- ✓ Because you really need the money, either for essential items or as a means of debt reduction.
- ✓ Because you have a particular talent, or a great idea, and you'd like to share it with others.
- ✓ Because you have certain dreams or goals for your family that cannot be accomplished any other way.

When you make the decision to give it a try, be sure to start small and avoid going into any kind of debt. Plan to put all profits right back into the business for the first three years. Do not start out by renting a building or by purchasing expensive materials. In any business, the first thing to do is to build a client list, and that can only be done by interfacing with people, one at a time. After awhile, your efforts to expand will pay off. In the beginning, do everything small, and don't expect to wind up swimming in profits right away.

I would also suggest that you put off any thoughts of running a home business until you are done having babies and toddlers. If you are starting really small, and are convinced you have everything under control, it may be okay to begin when your last child is still little. However, be careful that you don't impose too much on your older children. You don't want to turn your older daughters off to motherhood permanently by asking them to babysit the others constantly.

I did do a little preparation for the future while I had small babies. In an attempt to create a better future for myself and for the family, I spent those years going to school one night a week. However, that involvement had built-in limits. My husband was also very supportive. Without his support, even that limited schoolwork would never have worked. There is a reason that my business is just now getting a little more serious. My youngest son is now six years old. Before he was that age, I didn't feel comfortable going to large curriculum fairs or flying around the country. Now that he is a little older, I have more options, and can gradually begin to expand.

Finally, once again, *do not go into debt*. Do not risk family assets on anything risky. Once in awhile, with the support of your husband, it may be okay to risk some family savings, but be very, very conservative. There are so many ways to lose money in the business world that it can be mindboggling. One of the best ways to lose money is to blow it on advertising. Before spending any money on advertising, always see if there is some free way to get your word out. You may be able to get someone to write an article about your new business, or barter some kind of advertising for something else. Sometimes I write letters to advertise a workshop, and can get much more "bang for my buck" by using personal letters than an impersonal ad. Whatever you do, don't believe the commercials that tell you that simple ads really bring in lots of money. The only people who become rich using simple ads are the people who create those courses on television.

Above all else, do not borrow money from anyone outside the family. This is not Biblical, and it is not smart, and you will be very, very sorry!

Make Haste Slowly!

Finally, remember that everything good, including lifting yourselves out of financial difficulty, happens slowly and steadily. Any "get rich quick" schemes are bound to fail. Amassing a lot of money is probably not a very sound scriptural goal, anyway. However, having a prosperous future, where you will be able to meet the needs of your family adequately, is obviously a worthwhile goal.

When our children were younger, I didn't feel much need to have a lot of money. Roy had a decent job and we were able to get by, although we did buy a lot of garage-sale clothes, and frequented the consignment shops. (And yes, I did shop with coupons and go to day-old bread stores.) However, as the children started to get older, and there were expensive lessons and college tuition to think about, we started to need more money. I also had a dream of starting a retreat center out in the country for fellow homeschoolers. I knew that all of those dreams would require a great deal of money.

I started to study how rich people got their money. Very few people become wealthy through working for others on a salary. I began to realize that there were only a few ways to create wealth. The first was to inherit it. I knew we weren't apt to get too rich through that avenue. The second was to make money with money, through the stock market and other investment schemes. Since we didn't have much money to make money with, that didn't seem too plausible, either. The third was to make money through being an owner of something – land, houses, etc. That course of action appealed to me, but I didn't have any resources to start out with, and I didn't believe in the "no down payment" schemes, which involve heavy-duty mortgages and debt burdens. That left just one option: a business of my own. Once I decided on a goal and got motivated from a few loving, but biting words from my husband, I was able to set some goals and get started on the road to making my dreams come true.

I hope you are also able to move forward, out of debt, out of adversity, away from spiritual warfare, and on towards the establishment of a joyful Christian home school. Just remember, none of us are perfect, and none of us are able to all we would like to do with our lives. The key is to find a balance of contentment and forward drive, and learn to enjoy life in the present while we "press on towards the mark." (Phil 3:13-14) In the words of the insurance magnate, A.L. Williams, "All you can do is all you can do, but all you can do is *enough.*" I have repeated that statement many times during the last four years, and it has proven 100% true.

I had the strangest sensation when writing this book. I felt like I was really writing it to myself. Sometimes, during the writing, I would feel discouraged or overwhelmed. Then I would pick up the book, read through a particular section, and wind up ministering to myself! I hope that the book has a similar effect on you. Just remember, I don't have everything together all the time, either. None of us does. Any homeschooling mother who pretends that everything is rosy all the time is denying reality, but that shouldn't stop us from being joyful mothers, anyway! I hope that this book steers you in the proper direction so you can find the relaxed, joyful existence you are searching for, but always remember that the best "how to" book ever written has always been the Bible. If you are still searching for answers, that's the place to look.

Pass the Mashed Potatoes...

During the time I was working on this book, the last of our children turned his life over to Christ. It occurred to me that, from now on, all the rest will be gravy. The most important goal of all, within our family, has been met. If any of you still don't know Jesus in a personal way, and have become intrigued with meeting Him through the pages of this book, take heart! He's easy to find. All you have to do is search for Him with all your heart, and He will come into your life and fill you with satisfaction and joy. As for me, *"I have no greater joy than to hear that my children walk in truth."(3 John 1:4)*.

To write to Mary Hood, or to request a free sample of "The Relaxed Homeschooler Newsletter," contact her at P. O. Box 2524, Cartersville, GA 30120. Mary is available to speak at curriculum fairs and also puts on several major workshops of her own, including, "The Relaxed Home Schooling Workshop," "Countdown to Consistency," and "Homeschooling with Joy." Call or write to arrange a workshop in your area. She also speaks on a variety of shorter topics and many of these talks have been captured on audiocassette. While in the Atlanta area, stop in at the "Relaxed Home Schooler's Resource Center", which features enrichment classes for older students, parent workshops, a lending library, a curriculum lab, and new and used resources. As a homeschooling mom, Mary keeps irregular hours, so be sure to call (770)917-9141 before coming. Mary will try to answer individual questions submitted in writing, but please hold phone calls to a minimum, so she can continue to feel joyful and relaxed at home!